James Edward
OGLETHORPE

James Edward
OGLETHORPE

Joyce Blackburn

Dodd, Mead & Company

New York

To Lilla with love

1 2 3 4 5 6 7 8 9 10

LIBRARY OF CONGRESS CATALOGING IN PUBLICATION DATA

Blackburn, Joyce.
James Edward Oglethorpe.

Summary: A biography of the English founder and first
governor of the colony of Georgia who was active in
politics and penal reform and a supporter of the
American Revolution.
1. Oglethorpe, James Edward, 1696-1785 — Juvenile
literature. 2. Georgia — History — Colonial period, ca.
1600-1775 — Juvenile literature. 3. Georgia — Governors —
Biography — Juvenile literature. [1. Oglethorpe, James
Edward, 1696-1785. 2. Governors. 3. United States —
History — Colonial period, ca. 1600-1775 — Biography]
I. Title
F289.037B55 1983 975.8'02'0924 [B] [92] 82-23498
ISBN 0-396-08158-4

ACKNOWLEDGMENTS

IT WAS MY good fortune to have the cooperation of the U.S. Park Service at Fort Frederica National Monument, which houses the invaluable Margaret Davis Cate Library. Mrs. Ruby Berrie, retired curator of the Library, suggested numerous publications to aid my research. Of these, *James Edward Oglethorpe's Parliamentary Career* by Horace Maybray King (a monograph sponsored by the Committee on Faculty Research at Georgia College, Milledgeville, 1968), Amos Aschbach Ettinger's *James Edward Oglethorpe Imperial Idealist* (Clarendon Press, Oxford, 1936; Archon Books, 1968), and *Manuscripts of the Earl of Egmont* (His Majesty's Stationery Office, 1920-23) provided contemporary quotes from London newspapers and parliamentary records.

My cherished friends, Mrs. Burnett Vanstory and Miss Bessie Lewis, well known for their writings on South Georgia history, generously shared their knowledge and contributed to the accuracy of this record—as did Dr. Thinizy Spalding, specialist in Colonial History at the University of Georgia, Athens. Mrs. Lilla M. Hawes, Director of the Georgia Historical Society, Savannah, not only guided me through the mass of material on Georgia's beginnings collected by the Historical Society but saved me from perpetuating many errors.

I express sincere appreciation to all of these. And to my discerning companion-critic, Eugenia Price, with whom I relive America's history every day.

JKB
St. Simons Island, Georgia
17 March, 1970

He founded the province of Georgia; absolutely called it into existence; lived to see it severed from the empire which created it and become an independent state.

—EDMUND BURKE

Part One

1696 – 1732

CHARLESTON

OGEECHEE R.

SAVANNAH R.

BEAUFORT

Northern Line of Spanish Claim

SAVANNAH

ALTAMAHA R.

Ossabaw Is.

St. Catherines Is.

Sapelo Is.

SATILLA R.

DARIEN

FORT FREDERICA

St. Simons Is.

FORT ST. SIMONS

Jekyll Is.

ST. ANDREWS FORT

Cumberland Is.

FORT WILLIAM

ST. MARYS R.

ST. JOHNS R.

FORT ST. GEORGE

FORT DIEGO

ST. AUGUSTINE
CASTILLO DE SAN MARCOS

FORT MATANZAS

ATLANTIC OCEAN

Chapter 1

UP, UP, UP he climbed, taking the steps two at a time. His breath came short and quick, his legs trembled and felt weighted, but he kept climbing, glancing back down the steep stairwell which echoed with the sound of his boots on the stone. No one had followed . . . no need to hurry. He was almost at the top . . . twelve more steps. Push open the door . . . here, he was out into the air, free and alone. Jamie leaned against the parapet and rested.

Above him soared the spires of Magdalen Tower. Below, the reflection of the tower floated on the placid surface of the River Cherwell. It was almost sundown, normally the quiet time of day. At a right angle to the river, ran High Street, the main thoroughfare of Oxford, anything but quiet now. Boys were spilling from all directions—from doorways, from windows, from behind hedges—to surround a knot of their fellow students who marched waving scarlet banners and chanting, "Long live King George! Long live the King!"

From his vantage point overlooking the river, Jamie knew the marchers were about to be outnumbered and halted by a crowd of student Jacobites who had tried to get him to join them. "Come on, Jamie," his classmates had urged only moments ago. "You're one of us, and we're not going to allow the Constitution Club to demonstrate, are we?"

The Constitution Club was made up of Royalists. There were few of them on campus compared with the numbers of Jacobites who wanted the exiled Pretender, James II, restored to the English throne. The Royalists, on the other hand, supported the recently crowned monarch, George I. And this was May 28, 1715—His Majesty's birthday.

Why not let the Royalist students celebrate? Wasn't that their right? Was their loyalty to the King a threat to the Jacobites' freedom? Jamie knew his mother had entered him at Oxford because it was a Jacobite stronghold, but must he take sides? To prove his political heritage, did he have to riot? That was what the struggle down there in the street would turn into—a riot. He was sure of that.

Already the chants of the Royalists were being drowned out by the Jacobites' curses and obscenities. Already the shouts were angry: "Away with the Monarch! Away with the fool!" What had been teasing laughter turned into jeers; pushing and shoving into out-and-out combat. Jacobites grabbed the cravats of their enemies, twisted until the Royalists gagged and choked. They belted the banner-bearers with garbage, clubbed them to the ground, spit on them, kicked them, stamped on their flags, ripped them into shreds.

Suddenly, orange flames stabbed the rosy twilight—flames that shot high above the grappling bodies. The Jacobite students were burning an effigy of the King! How senseless it all was, Jamie thought; what a stupid climax to all of the violence. Less than a month ago, early on the morning of May Day, some of those very fellows stood here where he was standing and sang the traditional plainsong:

Sion, praise thy Saviour, singing
Hymns with exultation ringing,
Praise thy King and Shepherd true.

The contrast sickened him. How can I be proud of being a Jacobite, he asked himself? How can I support a majority in my college who force their views on others, who resort to brute power against their opponents?

As the fire hissed and leaped skyward, the bell known to all Oxford men as Great Tom began tolling curfew. The crowd which had gathered quickly on signal, now scattered, leaving the injured to crawl and limp away in its wake.

Jamie slowly retraced his steps down the silent tower stairwell and crossed the quadrangle to his rooms. The outraged night was eerily peaceful. Oxford would sleep.

One eighteen-year-old student named James Edward Oglethorpe would not.

There had been Oglethorpes at Oxford for at least four generations, but this fact probably influenced Jamie's opinion of the place very little. He found the curriculum limited, taught by professors uninspired by the standards of such illustrious predecessors as Erasmus and Samuel Pepys. He knew many of the faculty were lazy, devoted more to drink than to scholastic pursuits.

Mathematics was still suspect. Medical courses consisted mostly of lectures; dissection was forbidden. While Oxford boasted a Christopher Wren architectural masterpiece, the Sheldonian Theater, it seemed indifferent to libraries, and the books it did provide often moulded from neglect. Politics was far more emphasized than learning. It mattered less that Jamie was a good student than that he was the son of fervent Jacobites.

He remembered that his father had been indulgent and charming, but he had died when the boy was only five. Lady Eleanor Oglethorpe kept her husband's political and military exploits fresh, making him more dashing perhaps than he had been in reality. From lieutenant colonel in the King's Guards, Sir Theophilus had risen to a seat in Parliament, was knighted and described as a spoiled favorite in the Court. His rivals admitted that he was courageous and adventurous, but they also accused him of incompetence, arrogance, and bribery.

It was true that Sir Theophilus had been acquitted of murder when a less influential man would have hanged. It was true that he had been awarded valuable property for his services, including the family estate, Westbrook, in the borough of Haslemere, Surrey. He had killed at least three opponents in duels and was known to be an extravagant gambling partner of James II.

When King James, the Stuart Pretender, was driven by William of Orange to France where he set up the Jacobite Court at Saint-Germain, the Oglethorpes remained faithful in spite of the risks, and were later accused of conspiring to help James restore the Stuart reign. Eventually, James rewarded that faithfulness with ingratitude and cruel rejection. Being both wise and practical, Sir Theophilus and Lady Eleanor cast themselves upon the mercy of King William who "forgave" them and promptly enlisted Theophilus in his military campaigns.

With wily discretion, Colonel Oglethorpe overcame

12

the suspicion of his old critics and served with distinction in Parliament, adding meanwhile to his financial and social fortunes. By the time his last son, James Edward, was born, he was almost fifty. Even his associates said he had "settled down."

Jamie knew his mother was far from settled. She still spent more time in France, active in the exiled Court of the Pretender, than in England. Behind her back, gossips whispered that she was a spy and a heretic. Lady Eleanor ignored them, caught up in the intellectual ferment of the time. Unlike most women, she was able to debate the complex political and philosophical issues that attracted the important men who flocked to her drawing room. Her circle of friends included Jonathan Swift, the political satirist, who in 1713 began publishing the *Guardian* with the help of the essayist Addison. Other writers, among them Steele and Pope, were in the celebrated company invited to Lady Eleanor's. She must have had a way with men, so many of them became pawns in her Jacobite intrigues. From the earliest years of childhood, Jamie Oglethorpe knew great men of letters, government, and the military. And he sensed his mother's influence over them.

How Eleanor Oglethorpe found time to rear seven children following her husband's death is an amazement, but she was a devoted mother who suffered the same disappointments and heartbreaks of more ordinary women. Jamie's oldest brother, Lewis, died from a wound received in one of Marlborough's battles on the continent; Theophilus, Jr. was sent home from Madras in disgrace; Anne, who with her sister Ellen, attended school in Paris, was indicted for "converting a young woman to the Roman faith" (Lady Eleanor arranged a pardon); Fanny and Molly had been sent to

France also where they were expected to make advantageous marriages. All four of the sisters were Jacobites, popular in the Pretender's Court.

Now Lady Eleanor's hopes and ambitions were focused on Jamie, her youngest, and he knew she expected him to advance her political interests. But the radical Jacobite students he had observed at Oxford must have left him with misgivings.

Judging from his democratic leanings in later life, that was not the only thing which troubled him at Oxford. Sons of noblemen, and he was one, enjoyed superior treatment at the university. They ate at tables reserved just for them in the dining halls where they were served by commoners. In the town coffeehouses, his class of young gentlemen was shown preference at card games and cockfights. Jamie had become bored with his fellow aristocrats strutting self-consciously about Oxford in their stylish coats and breeches, embroidered waistcoats, and silk stockings. Some of their periwigs were so lofty they had to carry their black beaver tricorns rather than wear them.

Such dissatisfactions were cause enough for James Oglethorpe to drop out of college and begin a search for a more adventurous career abroad.

Chapter 2

"BUT, MOTHER, I'M tired of lectures and theories and outdated plays and political clubs. I'm tired of school—of old Oxford! Can't you understand that?" Jamie looked at Lady Eleanor pleadingly, but she did not seem to notice. Her gaze was following a pair of swans on the artificial lake. Young Oglethorpe and his mother were walking toward the rosary in one of the many formal gardens belonging to James II's magnificent Saint-Germain chateau.

"What I understand, Jamie, is that the pains I took with Bishop Hickes to gain your admission to Oxford were for naught." She turned suddenly and smiled. It was a disarming smile, still it made Jamie feel guilty. She had a way of doing that.

"You're disappointed in me, aren't you?" he asked.

"Not as disappointed as I am determined, my Son. Now that you have come to Paris, you will enroll in the Academy and continue your education."

"Why?"

"Must you ask why, Jamie? Isn't it bad enough that your brother Lewis died in the spring of life and that Theo has shown himself incapable of succeeding Lewis as head of the family, and—?"

"Where is Theo, by the way?" Jamie interrupted.

"In Sicily, playing the role of self-appointed diplomat with imprudent zeal." Lady Eleanor sighed, took Jamie's arm and led him off the path toward the edge of the lake.

"In other words, Mother, it's up to me," Jamie said flatly.

"It is your highborn privilege to add luster to your own father's name in Parliament, and education will scarcely be a handicap when the time comes for you to take office."

Jamie knew there was no point in trying to change her mind—not then. He had the same streak of tenacity and stubbornness. He also had her cunning. Even as he

15

changed the subject to the new wing being added to the royal stables, a plan was forming in his mind.

If he could not convince his mother that there were more exciting things for a young man to do than go to college, he knew someone who could. Hadn't she insisted that his patron be her distant cousin the Duke of Argyle? And wouldn't the Duke be useful now? She had always shown inordinate respect for Duke John's opinions and for no better reason than that he shared her Irish ancestry!

At once Jamie posted a letter to the Duke, explaining his desire to leave the Academy (against his mother's will) in order to enter military service. Could the Duke propose such a change to Lady Eleanor, stressing the illustrious military records of generations of Oglethorpes? "And don't forget to mention our Yorkshire ancestor who 'withstood William the Conqueror to the face,' and my grandfather who defied the dictator, Oliver Cromwell, in public."

The Duke of Argyle replied immediately that he was delighted to be a partner in Jamie's plot. "But it may take some time to find an appropriate post for you. My suggestion is that you attend Academy classes until I can make a suitable recommendation to your mother."

Some months later, Jamie, whose innocent expression hid the pulse of anticipation he felt, listened to his mother as she read aloud a letter from her cousin, Duke John. She had summoned Fanny and Molly to hear it, too, since it was bound to contain the latest London gossip and inside news about the Court and Parliament.

Finally, Lady Eleanor came to the part of the letter for which Jamie had been waiting:

"I understand, my dear Eleanor, that Jamie is there at Saint-Germain with you and the girls. He came to mind when I received an inquiry from Prince Eugene of Savoy about a suitable young officer who might serve him as secretary. You know that His Royal Highness shared with Marlborough the victory at Blenheim where he met your eldest, Lewis. And so the name of Oglethorpe is known to him. Since Jamie was commissioned Lieutenant in the First Regiment of Foot Guards before going to Oxford, it occurred to me to recommend him to His Royal Highness. Being a member of the Prince's entourage would provide your son with excellent executive experience and spare him from the more dangerous hazards of the battlefield.

"I shall await your decision in the matter, depending upon whether or not Jamie is sufficiently interested."

Jamie did not hear the remainder of the letter. In his excitement, he almost failed to realize when his mother finished reading. Then he heard his sister Fanny ask, "*Are* you sufficiently interested, Brother?"

From the look of pride on her face and the faces of Molly and his mother, Jamie knew his scheme had worked.

"Just think of our own Jamie in the service of the Prince of Savoy," Fanny exclaimed. "He's one of the greatest commanders of all time!"

"And a noble patron of the arts," Molly bubbled.

Jamie knew his mother expected him to comment, but he appeared to be studying a tapestry on the far wall, and waited for her to speak.

"This decision concerns only your brother, girls," she said. "Well? How shall I answer our cousin, Jamie?"

Her heavily-lidded gray eyes were forcing him to look at her now. He hoped she could not read his mind. "It

will mean leaving my studies at the Academy, Mother,"
he said guardedly. "But it does seem like the opportunity of a lifetime. Don't you feel that's the way Father
would have looked at it?"

Recalling how indulgent her husband had been with
his last born, Lady Oglethorpe, a wistful tone in her low
voice said, "Yes, your father would have thought it an
honor to serve with the Prince."

Chapter 3

PRINCE EUGENE'S CAMPAIGN against the Turks provided
James Edward Oglethorpe the military experience and
daring action any young man of that period would have
envied.

In 1701, a Grand Alliance had been formed in which
two naval powers, England and Holland, joined with
Emperor Leopold I (king of what was then known as
Bohemia and Hungary) to prevent the union of the
Spanish and French monarchies. Eugene, Prince of
Savoy, was the Imperial general in the Grand Alliance;
John Churchill, Duke of Marlborough, was the English
general.

Together, these leaders became heroes in the famous battle of Blenheim. Marlborough's glory was
short-lived. Within a decade, his political enemies
branded him "the butcher" and accused him of embez-
zlement for which he was driven out of office and replaced as commander-in-chief. During his associate's
decline, Eugene went on fighting, the wars ranging
over much of central Europe. By 1716, he was battling

the Turks whose Ottoman Empire had become a menace from the east. Young Englishmen spoiling for active training, volunteered for Prince Eugene's continental army.

Although little is known about Oglethorpe's six months under Eugene's command, it was not long before he was promoted. From a minor secretary to the General, James rose to aide-de-camp, proof that he quickly won the approval of the great, severely exacting Commander. Such a position allowed the young assistant to observe the genius of his superior firsthand. It also required him to pass fearlessly from one division to another communicating orders "with alertness and fidelity."

One of James's letters to his sister Fanny revealed that he fought with the troops in the "very bloody and sharp" battle of Belgrade. There, Prince Eugene decisively defeated the Turks. Belgrade could not have been the only battle in which James participated, because by the time the war ended, his military reputation was "outstanding for one so young." He was twenty.

In later life, Oglethorpe's memory for the details of Eugene's campaigns amazed his friends. Oddly, his favorite story demonstrated a skill in diplomacy rather than in arms: While at dinner with Prince Eugene and a company of other soldier-noblemen, James was seated beside the Prince of Württemberg, who not only emptied his wineglass with astonishing frequency but persisted in making uncomplimentary remarks about Britons. Being the youngest man at the table and the lowest ranking officer, Oglethorpe did not dare respond. But when the tipsy Prince suddenly raised his glass in his left hand and with his right "filliped" half of his wine right in the aide-de-camp's face, James could no longer ignore him.

This was at a time in history when a man considered it his moral duty to defend his honor in one way only —by dueling. Obviously, the Prince's action was a challenge to the junior officer—a contest with deadly weapons.

"I knew that any other man in that room would have instantly accepted the challenge," Oglethorpe said many years later. "And having been taken completely off guard, I was about to act in the customary way, but I didn't. In his condition, the Prince would have been an easy mark. The advantage was mine. Still, a mere glass of claret could not contain my honor, nor should it contain his life. I looked the Prince straight in the eye and smiled. 'That's a good joke, Your Highness,' I said. 'But we do it much better in England!' With everyone watching in uneasy suspense, I casually threw the whole contents of my glass into the Prince's face. The royal personage sputtered and coughed, dabbed at his eyebrows and beard dripping purplish red onto the front of his splendid uniform. The tension in the room gave way to laughter, the other officers congratulated me for pretending to take as a joke what the Prince meant for an insult."

After the war, James decided to travel. He wanted to visit his brother Theophilus who was living on the outskirts of Rome, and he planned to see the rest of Italy. Theophilus could not hide his surprise when he opened the door of his villa one day to the knock of the sophisticated, bemedaled young veteran. Could this be the baby of the family so recently an adolescent student?

Theophilus, on the other hand, had changed very

20

little, James decided. He was as fanatical about the Jacobite cause as ever, still fawning over the Pretender, who had repeatedly failed to gain enough political power to take over England's throne or to invade the country militarily. The old Pretender had tired and passed on his ambitions to his son, James III. He, too, failed. Fallen from favor even in France, the exiled Court, banished from Saint-Germain, had found a haven in Rome.

"You simply must have an audience with King James," Theophilus said repeatedly, and soon it was arranged for young Oglethorpe to meet the quasi king. Judging from a letter Theophilus sent his mother and sisters, the meeting was a success: "His Majesty told me today that he was well pleased with Jamie and that they have much in common. Can this mean Jamie is with us in our efforts to restore the throne of Great Britain to its rightful heir?"

When the dashing junior officer arrived in Paris, his mother and sisters were sure they, too, saw signs that James was a Jacobite. They would have been shocked to know that there was one thing only in his mind. He was sailing for England as soon as possible.

One day, over tea, he announced, "Mother, I'm going back to Westbrook."

Lady Eleanor hoped to keep her youngest child with her, but she recognized and respected the new maturity in his voice. The decision had been made without consulting her. She knew it was final.

"The family estate certainly needs attention, Jamie. It has, ever since your brother Lewis died. Theo's small talent for management has let it fall into utter neglect." Lady Oglethorpe hesitated, then said, "Westbrook, alone, is not enough to use up your energies though, just as it was never enough for your father. What else do you plan to do?"

"Get all of the estate affairs in order, meet the folk in the borough, establish myself in their favor, and when it is the right time, stand for Parliament."

How confident he is, Lady Eleanor thought. He is no longer a self-conscious youth. The tall slim body is hardened, disciplined, muscular. Those large gray eyes miss nothing. He has learned to conceal his awkward long neck with stylish close-fitting, wide cravats. Only the waspish waist and deep dimple in the chin remain boyish. My son is a man, taking charge of his destiny.

"Squire of Westbrook," she said, looking at him approvingly. "The title becomes you, Jamie."

"Thank you, Mother. Now, don't you think it's time for you and the rest of the family to stop calling me Jamie? Only boys are called Jamie. Squire Jamie Oglethorpe! That's pretty silly, don't you agree?"

They both laughed. "You're perfectly right, my dear," she said. "Squire James Edward Oglethorpe, Member of Parliament from Haslemere in the country Surrey. That sounds as it should."

But as she said the words, Lady Eleanor knew full well that if her son became the Haslemere representative in the English Government, he intended to pledge allegiance to George I, the King of England. In spite of her pride in him, there was a stabbing sense of defeat. He was not a loyal Jacobite after all.

Chapter 4

WESTBROOK, THE OGLETHORPE family estate, stretched westward from the banks of the stream after which it was named. On the other side lay the village of Godalming. The weathercock atop Godalming's medieval church steeple was a familiar landmark for travelers on the high road between London (thirty miles to the northeast) and nearby Haslemere.

From a distance, approaching as he did through acre after acre of lush meadow, James was reminded of the Watteau landscapes on exhibit in Paris, the vista was so serenely pastoral. At the same time there was something untamed about it. The very air of his homeland seemed wild and free, an indefinable aura no French painter could capture.

Massive and solid, the Westbrook manor house stared out from the steep hill at its back which shielded it from fierce north winds. Coming into view as the chaise passed through the ornate gates were vast parks and gardens, the servant cottages and the windmill, the family burial grounds. How unkept they looked now—how lonely. The winding drive was almost overgrown in places, brambles and fallen limbs startled the horses. There was no smoke rising from the four huge chimneys, but the lodgekeeper would soon have a staff assembled. There would be life in the great house again. There would be children playing on the wide lawn and terraces.

When they swept under the arching noble elms that

shaded the side courtyard, the driver slowed the horses and they clattered across the cobbles extending out from the doorway which opened from the manor hall.

It was the way he remembered—the thick stone walls of the ground floor covered by creeper, the two upper storeys bare and gray except where the facade was interrupted by windows, some large, some small.

At last I am old enough to understand my father's pride in this place, James thought. It was home to Father far more than to the rest of the family. Westbrook will be home to me now. I belong here.

James lost no time establishing himself as the new head of the House of Oglethorpe. Soon, the community around Godalming was abuzz with talk about the young squire's easy, friendly ways which contrasted pleasantly with those of the last master of Westbrook, the haughty Theophilus, Jr., whose defeat in his race for Parliament climaxed an unpopularity that sent him off to the continent never to return.

London papers began reporting Westbrook's glittering entertainments and political gatherings again; the farms began producing model crops. Up the hill behind the big house, James built an extraordinary wall, designed to shelter one of the largest vineyards in all of England.

Landed aristocrats and commoners alike speculated on the cost of the many improvements. "You have to give young Oglethorpe a lot of credit," they admitted. "He has brains and a flair for management." Even the children followed him through the narrow streets of the village hoping he would take them to Westbrook for games of blindman's buff, harry racket (hide-'n-seek), marbles, checkers, ball. With the older boys he spun humming tops, built flyer gigs, shot snipe, and sponsored tournaments in archery, his favorite pastime.

Archery had always been a hunting skill in England, and there was a time when the longbow was the main weapon in battles such as Agincourt, Poitiers, and Crécy, famous in English history. But not until 1676 did Charles II turn archery into a sport. From the time he could bend a bow, James Oglethorpe mastered all of its secrets—crossbow, target, flight, and field shooting. Once his young friends found that out, they begged him, "Show us how, show us!"

Intent and silent they watched him string the bow, fit an arrow (this is called "nocking") just below the knot or "kisser" in the string and draw it back until it almost touched his lips, then with hidden power send the arrow straight to the "gold" or bull's-eye of any target.

"Now let me, Mr. Oglethorpe, let me!" each youngster cried.

"All right, line up," James directed. "Take your turn. Did you know King Henry VIII was an expert bowman? He once made a member of his bodyguard a duke as a reward for winning an archery contest, probably because he had placed a large bet on it." James laughed, and the boys laughed with him.

Then with enthusiasm and much patience he taught them the primitive sport.

Once more an Oglethorpe was active in the life of Godalming and Haslemere. Once more, in the spring of 1722, an Oglethorpe became a local candidate for Parliament. Burrell and James ran on the Tory ticket; their opponents, Molyneaux and Blundell for the Whigs. For some time the Whigs had enjoyed a monopoly of power in the Government, but a disastrous financial speculation in the islands of the South Seas the year before turned the public against them.

The Whig party and all of England with it was threatened by ruin. Sir Robert Walpole, the only man capable of meeting such a crisis, came to the rescue. Furthermore, he became England's first Prime Minister, in the true sense, and established the cabinet and party system which would eventually modify the authority of the Crown.

In his first election, young Oglethorpe polled only one more vote than Peter Burrell, his fellow Tory. But together, they received twice as many as the opposing Whigs, who promptly declared the results had been rigged. Burrell and Oglethorpe were furious.

To make matters worse, the London *Daily Journal* ran headlines about the Whig accusations of fraud, and reported that "James Oglethorpe reacted with violence upon a chance meeting with the Whig secretary to the Bishop of London, Mr. Sharpe. The unstrung youthful candidate went so far as to draw his sword and wounded Sharpe in the belly!"

Oglethorpe replied to the accusations in a letter to the editor of the *Journal:* "Sir, an untarnished reputation is dearer to every honest man than life, and printing lies without the author's name is like stabbing in the dark. News-writers, in whose power it is to blacken the most spotless character, should have a very good authority before they publish things prejudicial to anyone's reputation." James went on to make it clear that the lies in the article were damaging and treacherous, and he asked that this true account of what happened be published:

"On Sunday the 25th (March) after Evening Service, Captain Onslow and Mr. Sharpe, meeting Mr. Burrell and Mr. Oglethorpe in the market-place at Haslemere, Mr. Oglethorpe tax'd Mr. Sharpe with some stories that

26

he had raised." Mr. Sharpe then warmly denied having said anything untrue. An argument developed, becoming so ferocious that Captain Onslow stepped between Oglethorpe and Sharpe. Instantly, Sharpe drew his sword. Oglethorpe and Burrell whipped out theirs, and in the scuffle, Oglethorpe wounded Mr. Sharpe "in the belly," and Captain Onslow in the thigh. The captain seized Oglethorpe's weapon, shouting, "Your life is in my power!" Oglethorpe shouted back, "Do your worst!" Struggling, he tore his sword through Onslow's hand, disabling him. "Then I bound up Captain Onslow's wounds and sent for a surgeon to tend him," Oglethorpe concluded. "These are the facts for the truth of which I appeal to Captain Onslow himself."

No contradiction was ever printed by the *Journal*. The incident brought out one thing, though. Politics managed what the Prince of Württemberg's insults could not—politics aroused in James a defensive, belligerent attitude. It was far more difficult for a man of importance at twenty-five, successfully launched upon a government career, to handle ridicule and slander. Like many fledgling politicians before and since, Oglethorpe was vulnerable to the muckraking of the press and to other pressures peculiar to politics which frequently corrupt a man's sense of tolerance and fairness.

In less than a month, another story appeared in the London *Daily Journal*, this time, certain of its facts. Having gone to London to take his seat in Parliament, James, heady with victory, celebrated—to excess. This happened in a disreputable house near Temple-Bar (the city gateway where heads of criminals were exhibited on the spikes of the gate) into which hackney-coachmen, shoeblacks, and linkmen were crowded.

There was so much confusion and noise, no one heard James's outcry, "I've been robbed. The gold piece I placed right here on the table in front of me is gone!"

Recklessly grabbing the man nearest him, he shrieked, "I've been robbed and here's the thief. Take him away!" Already angry that an aristocrat had invaded their preserve, the workmen rushed to the defense of the "thief," a linkman who began striking Oglethorpe with his torch.

"Give the bloke a cosh on the napper," the crowd chorused, joining the brawl. James outnumbered, drew his sword, and, according to the *Journal,* "gave the fellow a mortal wound in the breast, for which he was seized and carried before Mr. Justice Street, who committed him to the Gate-House."

The linkman died, and the newly elected representative from Haslemere was taken into custody by the constable. This would have put an end to the politician Oglethorpe had he not been cleared of the murder charges—presumably on the basis of self-defense. By October of that same year, 1722, a chastened James took his seat in the House of Commons and proceeded to make a more brilliant record there than any Oglethorpe before him.

Chapter 5

EVEN THOUGH HE had come close to ruining his reputation, James Oglethorpe was exceptionally honest at a time when the Prime Minister, Robert Walpole, said cynically, "Every man can be bought if the price is right." It was one thing to be cleared of a murder charge, it was far less common to be free of the suspicion of bribery and extortion. Because the personal integrity of Oglethorpe had never been questioned by anyone, he was a natural choice to serve on a committee investigating England's notorious debtors' prisons.

These were loathsome places where citizens were unjustly held for indefinite periods unless they managed to bribe their way to freedom. Wardens in these prisons sold their offices to the highest bidder much as one business man sells his business to another. For a price, wardens also arranged escapes, luxurious private rooms, epicurean meals. If a debtor was unable to buy such services, he received the most inhuman treatment. One warden, Thomas Bambridge, tortured his charges until they died so that he could collect their personal belongings of value.

The prisoners were not criminals. Many of them were respected persons who had simply overextended their credit, victims of the great depression which followed years of continental wars and government frauds. Prime Minister Walpole was so intent on the mammoth job of restoring stability and peace to the country that lesser social issues such as debtors' prisons escaped his attention.

There had been investigations before, unsuccessful ones. When Oglethorpe was appointed chairman of the prison committee, he determined that his investigation would force the reforms needed. For one thing, he would collect evidence himself. For another, he would take the committee directly to the scene. Once they saw conditions for themselves they would have no excuse for evasive, timid reports.

James's involvement in the assignment became far

more personal than official the day he visited his good friend, Robert Castell, in Fleet Prison. Castell was a well-to-do architect "of competent estate" whose creditors had thrown him into jail because he was not able to meet their demands. James found him languishing in filth and dampness, starving, weak with fever. Shocked that a young professional man like himself could be so brutally treated, James said, "Let me speak for you to Warden Bambridge."

"You'll just be wasting your breath," Robert Castell said bitterly. "Bambridge has managed to get my last shilling."

"What do you mean, your last shilling?"

"Well, at first I was able to buy a few meager comforts, such as a clean shirt and a shave once a month, but the warden kept raising his price for such favors until my funds were spent. Since then, he swears at me and threatens to put me in the spunging house where there's an epidemic of smallpox. The thought of it has given me nightmares every time I've been lucky enough to sleep."

"He wouldn't dare do that," Oglethorpe exclaimed. "That would be the same as murder!"

"My dear friend, murder is a common practice here. Bambridge has no conscience whatsoever. Every day he invents new refinements in the art of killing which I watch, and I say to myself, 'Will I be next?'"

All of the terror in the man's haunted eyes and trembling body were in those words, "Will I be next?" Suddenly, Robert grasped James by the shoulders. "Oglethorpe, listen to me! I so dread the thought of being in the same room with the plague, don't be surprised if my fear kills me before the smallpox can!"

Sickened with rage, Oglethorpe stumbled out of

30

Fleet Prison. Later, he learned that when Castell asked to be moved to another place, even the pleas of the warden's own agents did not move Bambridge. The promising young architect was placed in a room with the smallpox victims and in a few days, he died.

"The most debased criminal does not deserve such a fate," Oglethorpe protested when the news reached him. "To think, these prisoners are guilty of nothing more than owing money!"

In his first report on debtors' prisons to the House of Commons, James incorporated the tragic story of his friend Robert Castell. He also told of the case of Jacob Mendes Solas, a poor Portuguese, whom Bambridge kept chained in the Dungeon or Strong Room —a vaultlike cubicle in which the bodies of dead prisoners were tossed until the coroner completed his inquests.

"It has no chimney, no fireplace, nor any light," Oglethorpe's report read. "What adds to the wet and stench of the place, is its being built over the common shore and adjoining to the sink and dunghill where all of the nastiness of the prison is cast. In this miserable place the poor wretch Solas was kept by Bambridge, manacled and shackled for near two months."

The investigation was only beginning. From Fleet Prison, James took his committee to the Marshalsea where conditions were equally grim. "All last year there were sometimes forty persons locked up every night in a room sixteen by fourteen feet and about eight feet high. The surface is not enough to contain that number when laid down; so that one half are hung up in hammocks, while the others lie on the floor under them. Several have perished for want of air . . . they are forced

31

to ease nature within the room, the stench of which is noisome beyond expression."

The committee found prisoners crawling on hands and knees, too weak from hunger to walk, some delirious with fever and vermin. Mercifully, many died. But this led to a punishment that surpassed all other cruelties: The living were bound with ropes or chains to the dead; surviving debtors who were particularly displeasing to a warden, were tied to human carcasses and tossed in the yard.

"One man has been bound to two bodies for a week," the committee noted. "In that time, vermin devoured the flesh from the dead faces, ate out the eyes of the carcasses which were bloated, putrefied, and turned green during the prisoner's confinement with them."

At King's Bench Prison, they found the same starvation, torture, disease, exorbitant bribery, and death. Communicating its horror to Parliament, the committee proposed detailed reform of prison conditions and management, and under Oglethorpe's relentless prodding, won unanimous support for the Debtors Act, passed in 1730. For the first time in English history, the rights of a debtor were protected. Upon arrest, he was allowed twenty-four hours in which to raise money to avoid going to jail. Once he was there, he could petition against any wrongs done him. And bribery by any official was outlawed.

A twentieth-century Speaker of the House of Commons has said, "This law was perhaps Oglethorpe's greatest achievement as a member of Parliament."

Chapter 6

BY JANUARY, 1732, Prime Minister Walpole attained his national priority of peace by reaching an understanding with Austria and France and by signing the Treaty of Saville with Spain. In a speech which he wrote for the King, George II, to read before Parliament, Walpole predicted an era of tranquility in Europe. Oglethorpe could not share such optimism for the future. In the debate on the King's speech which followed, the Haslemere representative criticized the treaty with Spain: "How can we take such an agreement seriously as long as Spain continues to attack and rob English ships bound for the American colonies? We are permitted no revenge nor are we paid compensation."

While Walpole minimized the Spanish threat, it was obvious to his young critic that England must maintain a strong military defense. Another thing worried James. In the treaty with Austria, there was no provision for the safety of the Protestants in Salzburg where the Catholic monarchy was persecuting them. Both of these issues were of great concern to him.

Of equal concern was the collapse of the Charitable Corporation which loaned money at low rates to the poor. Shareholders in the Corporation demanded that Commons investigate. The financial leaders of the country along with many elected officials came under suspicion. Oglethorpe, with several others, stood above such corruption, and from his eloquent speeches before the House, it becomes clear that he was maturing into a moderate, truthful, wise legislator. His ability to see the whole picture beyond the small areas of local government which directly affected him made him even more rare in his day than he would be in the present.

"In all cases that come before this House, whether there seems to be a clashing of interest between one part of the country and another . . . the good of the whole is what we ought only to have under our consideration," he declared.

By the time he was thirty-five, James Edward Oglethorpe was perhaps the most prominent member of Parliament except for cabinet ministers. If and when the Opposition succeeded in ousting Walpole, here was a man with the experience and executive ability to take a key post in any new administration. The cutthroat habits of most officials who callously disregarded the good of common citizens made Oglethorpe stand out a champion of equality, justice, and tolerance several decades before Franklin and Jefferson.

The Industrial Revolution was still thirty years away, but he recognized the changes machines would bring and urged renewal of the patent on Sir Thomas Lamb's "silk engine" while others regarded it with superstitious dismay. With rare imagination and foresight, he introduced theories of Free Trade which would have abolished high tariffs and the Crown's protection of one colony at the expense of another. These theories turned out to be one hundred years ahead of the times. Unlike most of his colleagues, he shunned narrow attitudes, pursuing cosmopolitan and philanthropic interests that are still rated as liberal.

Two events during James's thirty-fifth year changed the course of his whole life. First, King George II signed a charter authorizing the establishment of a

34

colony in America between South Carolina and the Spanish territory of Florida "for the settling of the poor persons of London."

The second event was the death of Lady Eleanor Wall Oglethorpe. Carrying out her instructions, James buried his mother in the grave of her husband, Theophilus, near the altar of St. James's Church, Piccadilly. She had remained a loyal Jacobite, but her seventy years and the fame of her youngest son made it easy for Englishmen to overlook that fact. The public and press honored her. James was relieved and gratified to read in London's *Grub-Street Journal* that his mother ". . . was a woman of excellent memory and address, piercing wit, and solid judgment . . . indefatigable in serving her friends." That "she had courage and learning superior to her sex . . . ."

For three months James had spent every moment he could spare with her, knowing that the paralysis of her right side made the once dynamic woman feel only half a person, helpless, dependent. Now she was gone—the last meaningful tie with his family had been cut.

Through marrying titles, his sister Eleanor had become the Marquise de Mézières; Fanny, the Marquise des Marches of Piedmont. Molly was bound to marry just as well. With dubious authority, the Pretender king had made Anne, Countess of Oglethorpe and Theophilus a baron. Their lives continued to revolve around Jacobite affairs in Paris. They had less and less in common with their "very English" brother, James. There really was nothing to keep him from joining the colonial experiment across the Atlantic. A strange curiosity burned in his thoughts—could the issues for which he had fought in Parliament be proven practical and worthy in a new setting, in a new society unspoiled by inherited prejudice and debasing competition?

The following October, 1732, James Oglethorpe volunteered to lead a party which would pioneer the settling of Georgia.

Chapter 7

THE BOARD OF Trustees responsible for the administration and funding of the new colony was made up of men respected for their honesty and social conscience. Almost half of them had served on Oglethorpe's parliamentary committee which brought about the prison reforms. All of them were aware of the widening effects of England's great depression.

The Trustees lost no time in setting up weekly meetings and selected James's close friend, John Perceval, Earl of Egmont, as president. As they discussed their goals, three reasons for the colony became clear: "All of us are sympathetic to the poor and unemployed, but there are no jobs," one Trustee said. "The new colony will give these unfortunate but respectable people a chance at a fresh start."

"And once they are established and self-sustaining, their industry and success will bring much needed trade and wealth to the Crown," another suggested.

"There is a military reason for the settlement which may be the most important of all," Oglethorpe added. "Georgia will serve as a buffer between the southern frontier of South Carolina and the Spanish who have hostile Indians under their control. From the west is the French threat, but the Spanish are nearer, already governing the Florida territory. Because they scattered a few outposts and missions northward along the coast one hundred and fifty years ago, they are claiming that as well. The next thing we know, they will push on to Carolina, Virginia, Maryland . . ." Oglethorpe seemed to envision the whole Atlantic coast falling, colony by colony, to the old enemy, Spain.

Once it was decided why Georgia was necessary, the next step was publicizing the enterprise. Because of his extraordinary gift for communicating, James was given the job of making the new colony attractive to prospective settlers and financial supporters. It was equally important that he prevent any adverse publicity. The press, highly developed in London at the time, could sway the public either way—for Georgia or against it.

With his usual fervor James prepared an advertising campaign that far exceeded the publicity given any other English colony. In no time, Georgia became a household word. The drive for funds was successfully launched and applications from England's poor and Europe's Protestant emigrationists began pouring in.

Carefully, carefully the Trustees made their selections of those who would be in the first expedition to the "land of liberty and plenty." The most responsible and ambitious of the applicants were given preference —"all of whom had their creditors' leave to go, and none of whom were deserting wives or families."

Under Perceval's direction, the Government made every provision for the welfare of the volunteers. The Admiralty even notified British ships to give any needed assistance on the crossing. Robert Johnson, governor of the Carolina colony, prepared to welcome them to the new world. A distinguished chaplain, civil engineer, doctor, and apothecary were chosen to accompany the colonists, and there would be no stinting on supplies—food, tents, drugs, arms—everything needed for a frontier settlement.

The full company of travelers drove the rutted, slushy road from London to Gravesend November 15, 1732, all of the Trustees making the journey with James Oglethorpe to see him off. After all, was not he the moving force behind this hazardous venture? It was a bitter, murky day, and the warmth of friends was welcome. The wind blew off the Thames, threaded with sleet and snow, roughing the manes of the horses, whistling through the doors of the carriages.

Oglethorpe had spent the week at Westbrook, readying the family estate for his absence. Upon his return to London, he had found his colleagues as excited about his departure as he was. Today, on the way to Gravesend, the friends sharing his chaise did not stop talking, eagerly expounding their theories about what he would find in Georgia. James said almost nothing, watching the familiar views pass out of sight, realizing for the first time how long it might be before he saw them again. A melancholy mood blurred his spirit for a moment—in spite of his companions' rousing good wishes—for that moment he felt older and alone, already far from everything that had been a part of his life until now.

"Gravesend! Here we are!" Perceval, the Earl of Egmont, eagerly jumped from the carriage before the footman could help him. "There's the steeple of St. George's. Look at the splendid job they've made of rebuilding it!" The other men commented on the architecture, pointing out details to one another. "St. George's must be preserved because the Indian princess,

Pocahontas, is buried in the chancel. She saved Captain John Smith's life in the Virginia colony, you know."

"I pray there will be a Pocahontas in Georgia if I am in danger," Oglethorpe said. His friends laughed. James did not.

The Trustees in the caravan behind drew alongside and joined them. In a group, they walked to the waterfront where the 200-ton frigate *Anne* was docked, her sails and flags furled tightly, her masts groaning in the blustery November air.

Oglethorpe, along with the captain, doctor, engineer, and druggist would spend the night on board the *Anne*. So would 114 emigrants. (Four more sailed on the *Volant* which was loaded with freight.) The ship's master, Captain Thomas, hailed James and his party cheerfully, "If the weather doesn't worsen, gentlemen, we'll sail on the morrow." His stocky, short body suggested the solid, unwavering courage such a voyage demanded of a man.

Each family was called before the Trustees in the ship's cabin where they were asked, "Are you satisfied with the arrangements for your voyage and settlement? If not, it is not too late for you to change your mind. You can remain in London." Only one man, whose wife was ill, decided to stay.

The farewells were prolonged, the Trustees reluctant to leave their comrade to whom they had entrusted all of the authority of a colonial governor. None of them had accomplished more. None had been better born for a life of ease and its infinite refinements. Still, Oglethorpe was the one who, in the prime of life, volunteered to leave every comfort and cast his lot with unfortunates in a strange, untried climate—leaving

39

wealth and pleasure and esteem for the unknown—a wilderness inhabited by Indians and snakes. And at his own expense!

As he embraced his friends one after another, James Oglethorpe had never looked so splendid and manly. He seemed cloaked in a new dignity, a new grace.

"God go with you," his colleagues said.

"God be with us all," he answered.

Part Two

1732 – 1737

Chapter 8

THE AIR WAS still. The surface of the wide river shimmered undisturbed except for the scout boat pushing steadily upstream, its rowers sweating in the afternoon sun, their paddles almost noiseless in the clear water.

Two passengers sat alert and watchful in the bow—Oglethorpe and a Captain of Carolina Scouts. The Captain was experienced in colonial affairs, especially in dealing with the red man. He was bringing the newly arrived Englishman to explore this river named Savannah by the Indians. The party had made their way some ten miles from the mouth of the river searching for a town site which would be safe above the high-tide mark, on level, dry ground.

Though weary from travel and soothed by the vast silence of the wilderness through which the river wound, James Oglethorpe was tense, afraid some detail of sight or sound might escape him. The shore slipped by, a tangle of evergreen myrtle and bay and cedar casting patches of shadow darkened by the pines towering behind them. Birds and an occasional otter were the only signs of life. James was grateful that no one spoke. He felt he was almost dreaming. Could it have been less than a week ago that the sturdy *Anne*, lashed by the Atlantic's winter gales, had finally dropped anchor in Charles Town harbor? Two sickly infants had died during the passage, but the rest of the immigrants had revived quickly in the mild Carolina climate and the hospitality of Governor Robert Johnson, who, with his Council had voted to give the new settlers twenty barrels of rice, twenty-five hogs, 104 head of breeding cattle; they would also provide boats and ranger guides. "If anything more is necessary to further the success of this undertaking, I will do all in my power to forward it," Governor Johnson told them in his welcoming speech. Then he made a valuable personal gift of seven horses. The Charlestonians followed his example, donating everything that would be needed, even a drum, and a silver dish with spoon for the first child who would be born in the new colony of Georgia. Numbers of workmen said they would give their time and labor.

A party of scouts familiar with the coastal territory were assigned by the Carolina Council to accompany Oglethorpe south on the inland waterway from Beaufort (where the colonists were temporarily quartered), to Savannah Sound. Now they were proceeding inland, north and west. London, its weather raw and disagreeable in January, seemed many worlds away—its noise and crowds unreal. Here, Oglethorpe reveled in the air —clean, smelling of pine and sassafras; the sky above him—open, dazzling.

They were rounding a bend in the river when he saw the bluff—a high bank on the left, curving inward, forming a half-moon.

Pointing, Oglethorpe asked, "How high would you say that bluff is, Captain?"

"Forty feet, at least."

"From here, it looks flat on top. Could we climb up and take a look?"

"Certainly, sir." The Captain instructed his rangers to pull into the sandy shore. The climb was steep. So much the better, James thought, it could provide natural protection from tides and enemies.

He fould the bluff level on top, extending back from the river for as far as he could see. The site could not have been more ideal for the first settlement in his experiment.

Smiling, he said, "Captain, this place has been waiting for me to find it!"

"You and the Indians, sir." The Captain took a crude map from one of the rangers and unrolled it. "See, there's an Indian village near here. They call this Yamacraw Bluff."

"Yamacraw Bluff, so this is it!" Oglethorpe was surprised and pleased. "This is one of the Crown's oldest trading posts."

"Isn't this where John Musgrove lives?" a ranger asked the Captain.

"Yes, I believe it is. Some years ago, the South Carolina government sent Colonel John Musgrove into this area to negotiate trade with the natives. He married one of them. Their son, John, Jr., met and married a half-Indian woman who remained here with him. I think she's from up around Coweta, but she went to school in Carolina and speaks English. From all I've heard about John and Mary Musgrove, they're very enterprising and intelligent people."

"Yes, so I've heard and I must meet them," Oglethorpe said. "They will contact the Indians who live here for me." He knew that the Carolina Council had promised the Creek nation that no white settlement would be allowed south of the Savannah without the Indians' consent. If he brought his people here, there

45

must first be an agreement. "Let's find the Musgrove trading post."

Through loose, slippery sand the party made its way north along the bluff until they came to a clearing which had been made for several Indian farms and huts built of mud and wattle or twigs. In the forefront, nearest the river, stood a weathered-bark trade house, typical of those strung the length of the Savannah. Standing in the open doorway was a young woman who watched the Captain and Oglethorpe approach with obvious curiosity. She was only five feet tall, her hands and feet as tiny as a child's, but the expression in her black eyes was wise and old. Glistening braids of well-combed hair hung down long enough to be tucked into the beaded sash tied loosely around her waist. Just as Oglethorpe was wondering how best he could make himself understood, the woman spoke, her voice surprisingly mature, "You are looking for the trader Musgrove?"

"Yes," replied Oglethorpe. "Is he here—is this his house?"

"This is his house, but he is away." The woman paused. "I am Mary Musgrove, his wife. What is it you want here?"

"I am James Oglethorpe, Mrs. Musgrove—assigned by the King of England to begin a new colony in America, and I would like to meet with your chief to discuss a site, on the south end of the bluff there, for a settlement. My people and I have just arrived from London."

"My husband received a message to expect you."

"Now that I have spoken with you, I find myself hoping you and your husband will permit me to hire you as my interpreters and go-betweens with your tribe."

Mary Musgrove, her round face and regular features almost expressionless, thought for a few moments and

46

then said, "I will arrange a meeting with our Mico, Tomochichi. We are prepared to aid you in any way we can. Wait here."

From that day, Mary became indispensable to Oglethorpe. She had known many white men and her instinct and experience told her that she could trust this young Englishman. Only thirty, she was astute at handling her Indian people. She could persuade them to do what Oglethorpe wanted or she could turn them against him. There was something in his courteous and simple manner that suggested he was a true gentleman. And when he offered to pay her one hundred pounds annually for her services, she knew he had no plans to take advantage of the red man.

When she first told the village leaders about the visitors, their response was uneasy and wary, but they could sense that Mary wanted them to help the English. She quickly convinced them that a conference with Oglethorpe would be to their advantage, and they allowed Tomochichi to return with her to the trading house.

Oglethorpe waited anxiously. Would he be received in friendship? Governor Johnson had warned him that the Creeks had grown suspicious and afraid of the French and Spanish whites who had threatened their Indian people with torture and death. Would an Englishman be equally unwelcome? He knew it would take all the courage he could muster for the moment he met Chief Tomochichi that January day in 1733.

Though Mary Musgrove made the introductions formally, Oglethorpe was sure she was friendly. The Chief, graceful for all his great height and size, bowed low before him, and in spite of the differences of culture and color, there was an instant kinship. The educated, traveled, upper-class Oglethorpe with his Court associations, parliamentary successes, felt at home with the noble "savage" who seemed to him more regal than any English king.

He's a full size larger than I am, James thought. Well over six feet, all muscle, no fat. His skin is beautiful, a dark mahogany, his eyes light—gray like mine, the mouth firm but kind. I feel gratitude toward him—gratitude! I am a foreign intruder, but he is receiving me with generosity, in brotherhood.

As the two men, with Mary Musgrove's help, talked away the rest of the afternoon, James observed many things he had never seen before: The only covering for the chief's torso was a breech clout made of blue cloth, but he wore buckskin boots and leggings; at his side was a pouch holding knives and pipes and tobacco; his head was closely shaven except for a plaited scalp lock hanging over the left ear, in the other ear were several loops of copper; Tomochichi's body was naked from the waist up to a collar of rich brown otter skins.

That afternoon Oglethorpe learned that Tomochichi had been driven out of his Lower Creek tribe, not in dishonor, but over disputed authority. He was much older than he looked, having already lived a long life as a great warrior. When he had decided to found a settlement of his own, many Creeks and Yamasees followed him. "I am their father," the great man said simply. "And by the will of my people I am also a king, chosen by the larger community covering eight towns of the Lower Creeks. You Englishmen call those of us here, Yamacraws. I admire you Englishmen, and for you to bring your people to this place would benefit and educate us. Since the birth of my nephew, Toonahowi, now my adopted son, I have longed for him to learn English ways—your language and your religion. Now it will come to pass."

Tomochichi and Oglethorpe parted at sundown, friends, equals, secure in a respect so mutual it could only be deepened by years of association.

Chapter 9

WHEN OGLETHORPE RETURNED to Beaufort, South Carolina, three days later, the land for the settlement of Savannah had been selected with the consent of the Yamacraws who offered to help the colonists in any way they could. They *wanted* the English for Allies. It must have been with some pride as well as pleasure that James wrote the London Trustees, "A little Indian nation, the only one within fifty miles, is not only in amity, but desirous to be subjects to His Majesty King George, to have lands given them among us, and to send their children to our schools . . ."

The following Sunday Oglethorpe declared a day of praise and thanksgiving for the colonists' safe arrival in America. For the first time, the prospect of creating a new life was more than a dream—it was a promise as they prepared to travel once more, this time to their own colony. The *Anne* would be left behind at Port Royal. Oglethorpe had obtained a 70-ton sloop and five plantation boats to transport his people to the Savannah site. Delayed by a coastal storm, they did not arrive until February 12, 1733. Immediately, they began clearing land on the bluff where they would build their permanent homes.

Oglethorpe's tent was scarcely raised when a wide-eyed boy ran up to him yelling, "We're getting company! We're getting company!" Sure enough, Mico Tomochichi, his Queen, and John Musgrove were coming to welcome their new neighbors. Oglethorpe, more delighted than he dared show, invited them into his tent where they talked about what the Yamacraws could do to help the newcomers. When the Indians left, the English watched them go, waving good-bye.

The next months were filled with increasing activity:

FEBRUARY 15-

Divine Service of Thanksgiving was led by Dr. Herbert, the chaplain. Tomochichi and Queen Senauki, John and Mary Musgrove attended.

FEBRUARY 16-

Colonel William Bull, having been appointed by the Carolina Council, arrived with a party of workmen to assist in building the new town.

FEBRUARY 18-

Began digging trenches for 140 ft.-high palisades. A fire broke out. Pine tree near Oglethorpe's tent caught and had to be cut down. When it fell, it broke 2 barrels of beef, but the ammunition stored in Oglethorpe's tent was rescued before it could explode.

FEBRUARY 19-

Out of Public Stores, each family was given iron pot, skillet, 3 wooden bowls, copies of Bible, Common Book of Prayer, The Whole Duty of Man.

FEBRUARY 20-

Each person able to carry arms was given a musket with bayonet and cartridges.

FEBRUARY 22-

Colonists drawn up under arms first time; divided into Tythings, 10 men each; command of 4 Tythings assigned to Causton, Jones, Goddard and Gordon (whose journal provided this record). Sentinels appointed to guard edges of town; guard will change every 2 hours.
Frightening storm with thunder, lightning and "excessive hard rains" which beat through tents, soaking everyone to the skin. Oglethorpe orders 2 men to watch the river all night using large swivel gun since word came that a couple of robbers had broken out of the Charles Town jail and are coming this way.

FEBRUARY 23-

The robbers did not come. Felled trees are being cross cut in proper lengths for "clapp" boards.

MARCH 6-

The bell was hung.

MARCH 12-

Oglethorpe drove the first "pinn" in the first house to be framed and raised on the Square.

MARCH 23-

2 more houses completed; 3 frames raised; magazine ready; battery in place.

April 2-

A half-breed Irish-Indian came down the river. His actions made Oglethorpe suspect he was a spy for the Spanish at St. Augustine. He was put under guard but released for lack of evidence. Everyone excited.

APRIL 15-

After Sunday service, heads of Tythings were marched into the nearby woods. Oglethorpe ordered a target set up at 100 yards. "Every Sunday we will practice," he said. "There will be a prize of 8 shillings for the shot closest to the bull's-eye."

Setting an example of industry and cheerfulness, James had few moments to himself, acting as magistrate in all disputes, visiting anyone who became ill, serving on guard duty, and working alongside his people night and day, sharing their hardships. In fact, his care and supervision was so wholeheartedly paternal, most of the people called him "Father." (Some of the men called him Colonel though he had not been promoted.) He permitted no idleness; even the girls and boys were kept busy. James strode about briskly from one project to another, his energetic mind racing ahead to the next step of the plan for the town which he had drawn up, even before coming here. Only hard, back-tiring work could have accomplished so much in so short a time.

Steps were built from the river bank to the top of the bluff where his own tent stood under four giant pine trees. A crane and windlass helped unload the heaviest supplies. Homes were going up on the streets which he had laid out in spacious squares. At the south end of the town a guardhouse and a battery of cannon overlooked the river below. There would soon be a courthouse, a mill, a well, a church, and a building for the Public Stores. Savannah was sheltered from the southern and western winds by vast woods of pine trees, seventy to one hundred feet tall. He had planned every detail—now, he spent many hours recording what was done, what it cost, what was needed still. There was seldom time left for letters, but he knew he should keep the London Trustees informed about all that was going on in Savannah day after long day.

Sometimes he would pause to make little sermonlike speeches about the evils of rum, the debasement of slavery, both having been banned from the colony by his order. He knew some persons were resentful that the nearby Carolinians had plenty of rum and slaves. "It is my hope," he would say, "that through your good example this settlement may prove a blessing and not a curse to the native inhabitants."

Chapter 10

OGLETHORPE WAS READY to work out an agreement with the "native inhabitants" which would allow him to extend the Crown's influence west and south. The territory which most immediately interested him lay between the Savannah and the Altamaha rivers.

Between April and May of that first year in America, he had traveled to Charles Town where the Carolina Council received him warmly and after several days of consultations, sent him back to Savannah with 2,500 pounds, an indication of their enthusiastic support. And the Council agreed it was time to persuade the Indians of his plan for further exploration and settlement of their lands. From Tomochichi, he learned that the Lower Creeks and Uchees dominated all of the area stretching down along the coast between South Carolina and Spanish Florida.

Through Tomochichi, who was still considered a Creek leader, Oglethorpe invited the larger nations to send representatives to Savannah.

For the first time, they would meet the white Englishman whom the Yamacraws called "Father." Leading the party of Indians was a medicine man, dancing with a strict rhythm, spreading in each hand a large fan of white feathers to which were attached little bells, tinkling friendship and peace. Some fifty chosen Creek delegates, dignified and solemn, followed. A house had been prepared for the conference. They stared at the plank floor, then sat down on it crosslegged. Before them Oglethorpe sat on a high-backed Queen Anne bench, his interpreters on either side.

A tall, wiry Creek stood up to speak, and his voice had the tremor of great age. "Our land which lies southward from the Savannah was given us by the Great Power dwelling in the sky. He has given breath to all men. He has sent you to us in peace. We come to you in peace. The kings of our eight towns have agreed that the English may settle according to the request you have made through our Mico, Tomochichi. Together we bring a portion of our wealth that you might believe our good will."

Silently, in stately procession, the chief men from the eight Creek towns brought bundles of buckskins and laid them at Oglethorpe's feet.

"These are the best we have," the old Indian continued. "They are given with a good heart. We know your heart is good because of the way you have treated our kinsman Tomochichi and his people. He is a great warrior, a wise and courageous Mico who has long lived here near the tombs of our ancestors. You have not driven the Yamacraws out but shared food and learning with them. The chief men of our nation thank you."

Each of the eight leaders made similar speeches, then Tomochichi, with a Yamacraw youth, approached Oglethorpe and bowed. "My adopted son, Toonahowi," the chief said, motioning for the boy to step forward. "Show the great white friend our little present, Toonahowi."

The boy, handsome and princely, knelt to spread out an unmarked, black-brown buffalo skin.

"Turn it over," Tomochichi instructed. The boy flopped the big hide over as though it were a rug. Proudly he pointed at the head and neck feathers of an eagle painted there. "Explain to the great white friend," Tomochichi said.

"The eagle is a symbol of speed," the boy began. "The buffalo is a symbol of strength. You and the English are as swift as the bird and as strong as the beast since you fly over the vast seas to us and nothing can withstand you. The eagle's feathers are soft, a symbol of love. The buffalo skin is warm, a symbol of protection. We hope you will love and protect our families."

"In behalf of His Majesty King George and the British Empire, I thank you," Oglethorpe responded, visibly moved. "In settling here, the English do not intend to dispossess nor annoy you. Above all else, my prayer is for you to live in friendship. My desire to confirm a treaty of amity and commerce and obtain access to the territory described by the first speaker is secondary to a Treaty of Friendship."

It is not surprising that in such a favorable atmosphere, the convention with the Creeks ended with their ceding to England exactly what Oglethorpe wanted— the territory between the Savannah and the Altamaha "as far as the tide waters flow westward and southward, including the coastal islands, from Tybee to St. Simons." Ossabaw, St. Catherine's, and Sapelo, the first three islands south of Tybee, were to be reserved for Indian camping grounds where they could hunt and fish and bathe. The Creeks vowed they would have "no correspondence with the French and Spanish," nor trade with other than licensed British traders. The English agreed to set fair prices on the traders' goods. (A white blanket would be worth five buckskins; a gun, ten buckskins; a hatchet, three doeskins; a knife, one doeskin, etc. . . .) Any abuse of the agreement was to be settled by English law, an agreement "sealed with straight hearts" and in "true love."

After writing out the treaty, Oglethorpe gave to each leader a laced coat and hat (the lesser men received smaller presents), then he dismissed the Creeks in peace. His "judicious and honorable conduct" toward them was to prove more valuable to Georgia than its military defenses. From these earliest associations, the Indians knew that Oglethorpe "had no private end to gratify, no lands to secure for himself, no wealth to accumulate from them." Nothing in his background had prepared him to understand these aboriginal natives, and yet his dealings with them prove that he did. Without condescension, he was able to put himself in the Indian's place. And this at a time when class distinction, military rank, racial discrimination, and religious bigotry were all-important to most Englishmen.

The truth is, Oglethorpe found these supposedly "uncivilized savages" superior to some of the "Christians" who wanted to convert the Indians. Learning their language made it easier for him to appreciate their customs and manners. For example, the Yamacraws showed great respect for old people, they remembered any kindness "forever," they would not break a promise, and to them, generosity meant giving that which you wanted for yourself. They would not work for the Savannah settlers for pay—their labor was a gift to be shared.

One day while Oglethorpe was away from Savannah, a young Indian was found dead on the outskirts of the settlement. A brave ran to Tomochichi with the tragic news.

"How did he die?" was the chief's first question.

"He was shot," the brave answered. "We have few

guns, the English many. It must have been an Englishman who killed him."

"Is that your idea or did someone else tell you that?"
Tomochichi asked.

"The dead man's uncle, the powerful warrior, told
me."

Tomochichi went to the uncle who, in rage and grief,
was threatening to wipe out the white town.

"If what you want is revenge, take my life," Tomochichi said, baring his breast. "Take my life, kill me—for
I am an Englishman."

That brought the uncle to his senses, and it was later
proven that his nephew had killed himself in a fit of
despondency.

Tomochichi instructed his hunters to provide Oglethorpe and the colonists with food: trout, perch, catfish,
and rockfish were abundant as were wild game, especially turkey and deer. By July, 1733, Savannah was so
well provided for, its affairs organized so efficiently,
Oglethorpe decided he could entrust administration to
selected officials rather than direct all activities himself.

In spite of an epidemic of "fever and flux" which had
killed several colonists, including Cox, the doctor,
James set July 7 apart for a special thanksgiving celebration, during which he would assign responsibilities.

Early that morning, all of the townspeople gathered
before his tent on the bluff—at least 130 of them. After
prayers seeking divine guidance, James divided the
town into wards and assigned lots for the homes of all
freeholders. A Town Court of Record was established,
bailiffs were sworn, the first session of magistrates was
held, and the first jury was impaneled to try the first
case in the colony of Georgia.

While the ceremonies took most of the day, there was time for a great feast, provided by Oglethorpe. The settlers became more and more festive, realizing for the first time perhaps that they had survived fire and accidents, heat and rains, insects far worse than wild animals, brackish drinking water, death. Miraculous as it must have seemed to most of them, they were established landowners in the new colony—they were Georgians.

Chapter 11

EARLY IN 1734, accompanied by a Captain Ferguson and sixteen rangers serving under him, James Oglethorpe with two trusted Yamacraws set out for the southern frontier. With Savannah established, it was important to explore the rest of the territory he had claimed for the Crown.

Captain Ferguson said that the best route would be the inland waterway which passed along the leeward side of the coastal islands, winding through vast expanses of salt marsh where numerous creeks and the rivers Ogechee and Altamaha emptied into wide-mouthed sounds. Up the Ogechee, under Oglethorpe's orders, a fort had been built to protect Savannah from sneak attack. Oglethorpe said he wanted to stop there before heading south. He named the outpost Fort Argyle after his mentor, the Duke.

Though it was winter, the semitropical sun was hot during the afternoon, glancing off the black mudbanks exposed at low tides. By midnight the temperature could drop to freezing, exposing the party to cutting offshore winds and drenching rains. But there was something about the early morning air, when he awakened, that made Oglethorpe want to press on—a salty smell, part iodine, part soil, part decaying plants. It refreshed him. Striding up and down in the semidarkness, he supervised breakfast and the loading of the boats, so that the rangers could push off from the campsite into the current again even before the herons awakened to begin their dawn fishing.

"What is that?" he asked the Indians, again and again, as the shoreline slid by. Patiently they taught him to identify Spartina, the tawny marsh grass; the evergreen trees, live oak, slash pine, cypress, cedar; the winter-bare gums and nut trees; the lower fringes of palmetto, marsh elder, myrtle, cassina; grapevines and thorny wild roses. When they pointed out mounds of oyster shells higher than their heads, they recalled hunting and fishing parties that had lasted from season to season. They showed him the ruins of Fort King George on the north branch of the Altamaha before going on to nearby St. Simons Island. It did not seem to occur to Oglethorpe that he had passed south of the Altamaha River, the boundary which he had originally drawn for the Georgia territory. Not only had the Spanish claimed it first, he was now moving ominously closer to their fortifications.

At once he decided to make St. Simons a military base since its southern tip was an ideal lookout. "From here we can see anyone coming up the coast from Florida," he said. Another island lay close by and seeing on his map that it was known only by the Indian title Ospo, he named it Jekyll after his friend, the Whig politician, Sir Joseph Jekyll.

Returning northward along the western shore of St. Simons, Oglethorpe spotted a point of high land about halfway up the island where the river curved, somewhat concealing it. "Captain Ferguson, this is just the place for a fort, don't you think? It will give us far better defense against the Spanish than Fort Argyle," James said excitedly. "Of course, I'll have to convince the Trustees of that!"

He had intended going back to London long before this, but administration of the new colony had delayed him. Now that he had seen the coastal islands himself (and arbitrarily extended the Georgia border southward), it seemed urgent that he report to the Trustees in person and ask for further financial grants from Parliament.

At about the same time Oglethorpe took the exploring party south, the ship *Purrysburgh* left Dover, England, headed for Savannah. It arrived in March, bringing Salzburgers, driven from Austria, because they were Protestants. Oglethorpe, already sympathetic to their cause, was interested in increasing Georgia's population, particularly with settlers as industrious as the Salzburgers, and so he welcomed them.

Their leader was Baron Von Reck, an educated, diligent man who had much in common with Oglethorpe. Von Reck was equally eager to settle his people in a free land where they could support themselves and worship God as they pleased.

"You may stay with us here in Savannah or settle your own town, Baron," Oglethorpe told the Salzburger.

"You will have more people coming all the time," Baron Von Reck said. "Since we want to farm and become independent, another settlement might best serve us. But let us be near by."

"Good, I will have Tomochichi show you the best land available, and if you don't mind, I'll come along."

Some thirty miles inland from the sea, where there was a freshwater supply from natural springs, Von Reck selected a site. Tomochichi and James helped lay out a town which was called Ebenezer, a biblical name meaning "stone of help."

When Von Reck brought his people to Ebenezer, he declared, "It is edifying to us that we have come to the borders of this promised land this day, when, as we are taught in the gospel lesson, Jesus came to the borders by the seacoast after He too had endured persecution and rejection by his countrymen."

The colony of Georgia was fulfilling the dream of the Trustees; it not only provided work and safety for people who needed them, there was "mercy and charity for all."

James's plans to go back to England were delayed still longer by the settling of the Salzburgers, but finally the right time had come to leave Georgia. Savannah was growing, forty houses were up, the courthouse and Public Stores house completed. From a new staff near the guardhouse, the British jack flew, and profitable trees and plants were being cultivated in a public garden on the eastern rim of the bluff. An octagonal lighthouse, ninety feet high, was to go up at the mouth of the Savannah River, on Tybee. The first Georgian settlement was prospering as were the smaller surrounding villages of Highgate, Thunderbolt, Abercorn, Hampstead, Ebenezer, and Fort Argyle.

Oglethorpe, the founder, could depart with the greatest sense of accomplishment, certain that his report would not only be approved by the Trustees, but that it would persuade them to expand their holdings in the new colony. Just one thing troubled him. Why hadn't he written the Trustees more often? Why hadn't he found time to keep them informed of all he was doing? If there was to be any criticism, he knew that would be it. Suddenly, he felt almost as guilty about his poor correspondence as he felt about having spent most of his personal inheritance on the Georgia experiment. Would time prove it worth all the risks?

Chapter 12

OGLETHORPE WAS WELCOMED home with the same enthusiasm the Indians, Carolinians, and Salzburgers had shown for him back in Georgia. At least, the London newspapers and the royal reception led him to think so. Nothing in his warm welcome told him that some of the Trustees had grown indifferent to his cause, that others resented his failure to inform them of his intentions, and that all of them were worried about the constant expense of maintaining the Georgia project. James's close friend John Perceval, Earl of Egmont, had petitioned Parliament and pestered Prime Minister Walpole for further grants until a definite resistance was spreading. Without telling the Trustees how he had used their money, James had drawn many drafts on their funds. That, too, did not sit well with anyone.

But James had not known any of this when he decided to take along a company of Indians. Was there any better way to show the Trustees how humane and profitable their investment had been? Was there any better way to advertise the Georgia colony, to focus the public's attention on it? One can imagine the sensation caused by the red men in their native costumes, with the exotic, strange-sounding names—Tomochichi, Toonahowi, Hillispilli, Apakowlski, Stimalchi, Hinguithi, Sinlouchi, Umphichi. Even the Trustees and the Government could not resist their novel charm and childlike wonder at being in the great city of London.

The Gentleman's Magazine published poems in honor of Oglethorpe and his Indian friends. A medal was struck to commemorate the visit. A "grand entertainment" was staged by the Trustees who also launched a 250-ton ship christened *Oglethorpe*. One year in the colony had brought him more fame than ten years in Parliament. For days, bells rang, bonfires illuminated London's streets. Crowds followed the Georgia party from place to place, cheering James, trying to touch him and the Indians.

More surprising perhaps was the reaction of the Royal Court and English nobility. A periodical describes the way in which Tomochichi, his fellow chiefs, and their interpreter, were driven to Kensington Palace in three of the king's coaches, each drawn by six matched horses, right to the main entrance where the king's bodyguard took them to the Lord Chamberlain, who in turn, led them to the Presence Chamber where George II and Queen Caroline, sitting on their thrones, received the red "savages."

The British monarchs, in their bejeweled gold crowns, were not more regal and impressive that day than were King Tomochichi and Queen Senauki in their loose scarlet robes trimmed with gold lace, loaned to them for the occasion, which could not conceal the fur ties about their necks, the beaded buckskin boots on their feet. The other Creek officials wore blue and yellow and painted their faces in traditional designs for the ceremony. They chose Tomochichi to speak for them to the King.

Oglethorpe thought he had never seen his old friend look so tall, so majestic, even though the tattoos at the left corner of his mouth gleamed red and primitive against his dark skin. James knew they were marks of honor, of reward. It must have surprised those in the Presence Chamber to hear the eloquent words of the Indian ruler to the British Monarch: "I see the majesty of your face, the greatness of your house, and the number of your people," Tomochichi began solemnly. "I am come over in my old days, and though I cannot live to see any advantage to myself, I am come for the good of the children of all the nations of the Upper and Lower Creeks, that they may be instructed in the knowledge of the English."

Young Toonahowi, the adopted son of the aged chief, then came forward with a gift—a shawl of feathers, exquisitely designed. "These are the feathers of the eagle," explained Toonahowi. "We have brought them to leave with you, O great King, as a sign of everlasting peace."

King George, obviously moved by such brotherly warmth and kindness, expressed his pleasure with the gift and with the concord it symbolized. He concluded, "I shall be glad of any occasion to show you a mark of my particular friendship and esteem."

Oglethorpe's Yamacraw friends had taken England by storm, just as he knew they would, winning more popularity for the colony than any speech in Parliament or any London editorial. The Government voted twenty pounds for each Indian's weekly expenses. The Archbishop of Canterbury sent a barge to bring them to Lambeth Palace, his residence. Lady Dutry entertained them lavishly, as did other noble families. The famous school, Eton, honored them, and when Tomochichi suggested a holiday for all scholars, they cheered him. The Indians were given a tour of the royal quarters at Windsor and Hampton Court. Prince William (who would become the Duke of Cumberland), only thirteen years old, liked Toonahowi so much he gave the Yamacraw prince a gold watch. The throngs who followed the Indians all over London showered them with gifts which were valued at four hundred pounds!

When their ship finally set sail for Georgia, Tomochichi's party was both happy and sad; happy to have been received so heartily by the English, happy to be going back to the forests, but sad to leave their great friend Oglethorpe behind. He had been with them constantly for such a long time, even a brief separation seemed unbearable.

Chapter 13

ALONE IN LONDON, Oglethorpe was busy mending his fences. Gradually, subtly, he dealt with the various whispered accusations regarding his inefficiency and neglect. While he probably took no active role in the Government during his one-and-a-half-year stay in England, he did speak to the House of Commons in support of two policies he wanted enforced in the new colony.

One prohibited the importation of rum, brandy, and

other distilled spirits. (Ale, beer, and wine had been provided the settlers but were not considered harmful.) The other policy prohibited the importation of slaves.

With deep distress, James had concluded that Carolina traders were smuggling both liquor and Negroes into his territory on a large scale. Rum had brought disease to the red men and accounted for the misbehavior of many colonists. And, while he himself had learned moderation after his youthful excesses, he saw no better answer for the problem than prohibition.

At a time when slave trade was bringing huge profit to the Crown and supplying cheap, adaptable labor in England's colonies, Oglethorpe's attitude toward slavery was strikingly independent. That he had personally ransomed an intelligent Mohammedan slave, Job, was well known in London where Job had basked in the limelight of that city's society. Sir Hans Sloane, founder of the British Museum, had enlisted Job's expert help in cataloging Arabic manuscripts. As Oglethorpe had used Tomochichi to convince Englishmen of the nobility of the red man, so he may have used Job to convince the Trustees of the black man's right to freedom and dignity. The fact is, the prohibition of rum, brandy, and slaves was ratified by Parliament. So was the treaty which had been drawn up with the Creeks governing fair trade. These victories for James Oglethorpe's ideals "were so far in advance of conditions at the time and place as to be unpractical." They would become increasingly controversial.

While some of the Trustees remained dissatisfied with James's accounting of their funds, most of them thought the expenditure of his own fortune for the colony was proof enough of his honesty. An additional grant of 26,000 pounds was voted. Besides the money, he was given permission to enlist a force of fighting men from Scotland. (It was only practical, he told Parliament, to anticipate active hostile acts by the Spanish on the new southern border of Georgia.) He hired Lieutenant Hugh Mackay to recruit Scottish Highlanders, 130 of them, with their families, to settle along the Altamaha River boundary.

Famous for their courage and fierceness in battle, there could not be the disappointment in the Highlanders that the Trustees experienced with a company of Moravians sent to America. Being pacifists, the Moravians refused to participate in the defense of the colony, causing much dissension. Finally, most of them had moved north to Pennsylvania.

Another group created problems as well—forty Jews, who had gone to Savannah without the approval or consent of the Trustees. Oglethorpe defended them, declaring they would be a useful addition to the growing population which was becoming remarkably cosmopolitan. A few years after the founding of Georgia, Swiss, Salzburgers, Piedmontese, Welsh, Highlanders, and Jews had joined the English there.

King George shared Oglethorpe's vision of Georgia's potential. And, if the Queen did not, her mind was quickly changed by James's shrewd gift to her of thirty pounds of raw silk from the colony, which Queen Caroline had woven into a gown she proudly wore to her husband's birthday party.

There was no doubt that hearing about Georgia firsthand from its founder aroused fresh interest among the Trustees. With their renewed support, plus that of the Crown, Oglethorpe could leave again for America. The first difficult phase of founding and administering the colony was behind him. Ahead lay the next, a military one, if he chose to challenge the Spanish.

After giving an elaborate dinner for his sponsors and friends, he sailed on the *Simmonds* with 257 new settlers, the largest group yet. The passage could not have been more unpleasant. In spite of the devout prayers of the Wesley brothers, John and Charles, whom Oglethorpe was taking along to see after the spiritual needs of his people, the severe storms made everyone desperately seasick. Although weak from a recurring attack of fever contracted his first year in Savannah, James encouraged, even nursed the ill passengers. He could have ignored them and rested in his quarters. He could have had the choice food for himself. Instead, he was "always ready, night and day, to give up his own ease and convenience to serve the poorest . . . he seldom eats more than once a day . . . he gives his fresh provisions away." A prospective mother, expected to die, was moved to his cabin where he nursed her back to health.

This glimpse of James's humanity explains the esteem and devotion shown him by most of the colonists. Does it also explain his slowness to recognize treachery in others? While the Carolina Governor and Assembly welcomed him even more warmly than on his first arrival, and a twenty-one-gun salute was fired from the fort when he climbed the Savannah bluff, the first Georgia settlement was in an uproar. Everything looked "in good order," building had increased startlingly (two hundred houses), but the man left in charge during Oglethorpe's absence had stirred up a contagion of trouble.

Thomas Causton, bailiff and storekeeper, had been a disastrous choice to supervise Savannah town. Among themselves, the resentful colonists called him covetous, deceitful, proud, cruel, without conscience. It was common talk that Causton could not handle authority, it turned his head.

"He's a dictator, that's what, as bloody as any czar! *Now* he's threatening jurors who don't reach verdicts according to his orders."

"But worse than that, is the way he's going around saying we own neither our land nor our possessions. Even the public funds are not ours, and he'll use them as *he* pleases."

"I heard that after he mis-applied that last big donation from Carolina, the government up there said there'd be no more."

"Well, the Charles Town paper that came last week exposed all the mean punishments he's invented for minor misdemeanors, you know—stocks, 'n irons 'n gibbets 'n whipping-post 'n now the long-house. The paper says we ought to move to Carolina."

"I know of several folk planning to do just that!"

If Causton's victims were waiting for Oglethorpe to set matters right when he got back, they were bitterly disappointed. He remained in Savannah only long enough to inspect the garrison, hold a seige of conferences, and study a stack of reports. This kept him busy until one and two every morning, leaving almost no time for sleep or conversation with anyone other than officials, all of whom were under Causton's sword.

That he did not grasp the true state of affairs may have been due to the impressive outward growth of Savannah. Its six hundred citizens must like the place, he reasoned, and more were coming. Oglethorpe wished he could stay, but he felt he must get down to St. Simons Island as soon as possible to establish a new town now authorized by the Trustees, which might be-

70

come the most important point of defense in the whole colony.

On February 14, 1736, ranger captain Ferguson, a missionary named Ingham, and a few Indians left with Oglethorpe in a scout boat for St. Simons. The sloop, *Midnight,* loaded with workmen and provisions had gone ahead. James was in such a hurry, he kept the rowers busy through the night as well as the day, rewarding them with his own rations for their efforts in spite of the high winds blowing off the sea. Again and again the open boat was almost swamped, but the rowers pushed on to the mouth of the Altamaha where they sighted another boat.

As it approached, Oglethorpe shouted, "It's Mackay, the fellow who enlisted the Highlanders for me!"

"Welcome, welcome," Mackay called, delighted to see his commander again. "This is Officer Cuthbert, sir." The two brawny Scots saluted as they brought their boat alongside.

"I saw the smoke over there on the bluff, but I didn't know it was from your chimneys," Oglethorpe said. Turning to Ferguson he explained, "They're from the Darien district."

"Can you stop overnight with us, sir?" Mackay asked.

"No, Mackay, not this trip. I want to get on down to St. Simons. I sent the *Midnight* ahead, and if she's there, we'll get her unloaded before sundown."

"We'll be over tomorrow, sir, and help you." The Highlanders, jaunty in their kilts and bonnets, saluted again as Oglethorpe's boat was guided back into the swift current. Funny how reassuring it was, just seeing Mackay again. I'm positive the Scots and Indians are bound to be the fiercest fighting combination in the new world, he mused. Some Englishmen I know make fun of Highlanders for wearing their kilts and blowing their bagpipes. Some, on the other hand, think of them as barbarians. They are simply the sturdiest, most fearless race I've ever met. I expect to learn much from them. After centuries of guerrillalike warfare in their homeland, they are better prepared than I am for what may lie ahead. I wonder how long it will take the Spanish to learn we're on St. Simons.

"On the 18th we arrived at the island of St. Simons," the missionary Ingham recorded. "We were ordered to look to our arms, prime and swivel-guns, and make everything ready in case of attack." The *Midnight* was waiting to unload. Wasting no time, Oglethorpe set every man to work, and he himself directed the building of shelters for the stores and colonists. These were temporary structures of ridgepoles and rafters, thatched over with palmetto fronds.

Indians, friends of Tomochichi, brought game for the evening meal, and soon afterward the weary company drifted off to sleep. Everyone but Oglethorpe, who was wide awake, sitting up beside the campfire planning the next day's work. Just before dawn, he roused the workmen and distributed dried beef and cold barley biscuits to each, then he spread out on the ground the map of a town and said, "Right here is the fort. We will begin it today. Twenty of you will be assigned to the construction, ten of you to digging the ditch that must surround the fort, the dirt to be mounded up for a rampart. It's sandy, so the rampart must be turfed to prevent erosion." For each person he had a job in mind, and a deadline for its completion.

So the southernmost town in Georgia was begun under great moss-draped live oaks, overlooking the river and acre after acre of marshes. Oglethorpe named the town Frederica in honor of the popular Prince of Wales, Frederick Louis, as he had named the colony in honor of King George.

Chapter 14

NO ONE KNEW better than James Oglethorpe the hardships facing the Frederica settlers, and he went back to Savannah to recruit them, holding out no false promises.

"It will not be held against you if you change your mind," he told them. "I won't blame you for staying in Savannah, because life in Frederica will be harder than you can even imagine. It will also be dangerous."

By March, forty-four men and seventy-two women and children had begun life in the new town, Frederica. James carefully laid out thirty acres which had already been cleared and used by Indians. Each freeholder along the main street (Broad) was to have a lot 60x90 feet for house and garden, while the lots fronting the river were 30x60. Large public gardens were planted inland from the town for potatoes, barley, flax, corn, turnips, hemp, cucumbers, kidney beans, melons. A meadow was found for cattle, and most important, two wells were dug.

In less than a month, the fort, later named after the town, was completed except for one of the four bastions projecting from the corners of the simple square design. Near the north bastion, pointing into the river was a spur or elbow of land that made an ideal lookout. From it, anyone approaching by water from north or south could be spotted. A battery of cannon was mounted there, commanding the river.

Inside the fort, powder magazines and storehouses were built. Nearby, a parade ground was laid out, and at its edge, two tents were pitched for Oglethorpe's use. From Savannah and Darien workmen came to help the settlers. Mackay even managed to bring six horses and a plow by decking over several dugout canoes called periaguas.

Besides the *Midnight,* another British sloop, *H. M. Hawk,* anchored a few miles to the south. Its captain, James Gascoigne, had convoyed the settlers' Atlantic crossing. His orders were to establish naval headquarters on the island. The best place seemed to be a high bluff where the river channel was deep enough for several ships. (It was later named for the Captain, and he claimed a large tract of land there.)

The colonists had been chosen by the Trustees for their skills since Frederica was to be a self-sustaining community. Anyone visiting the site today where many foundations of the town have been excavated, will see the names of those early Georgians: Hawkins, surgeon; Davison, constable; Welch, carpenter; Allen, baker; Le Vally, shoemaker; Carr, Captain of Boatmen; Spencer, bricklayer; Cannon, carpenter, bailiff.

In time, the thatched "booths" were replaced by brick and wood houses. Some homes, including Oglethorpe's, were built outside the village and a group of Salzburgers established their German Village a couple of miles east. Within a short time Frederica was an industrious, contented society.

James seemed to feel more at home than at any time since leaving Westbrook. His frame cottage was surrounded by a 300-acre tract to the southeast, near enough for him to see the village and fort. The place became known as the Farm because of the large gardens and orchards and oak groves. They were much smaller than those at Westbrook, but they reminded him of his home county, rural Surrey.

Between the cultivated fields and gardens stood woods of live and water oak, cedar, holly, bay, pine— always green. In late autumn, sweet gums turned vermilion, the hickorys and bullis grapevines a clear yellow. Bears, squirrels, raccoons, wildcats, opossums, rabbits, and deer were plentiful in the woods. Wild turkey, geese, duck, and doves were everywhere; oysters were abundant, fish and crabs swept in by the tides.

Life was rugged, but such variety, such bounty and space surpassed the wildest hopes of those settlers who came from cramped and ugly cities. Frederica was not an Eden, though. Unfamiliar with the semitropics, the people were terrified by alligators and snakes that became more active as summer progressed. Mosquitoes, gnats, red bugs, deer flies, spiders, ticks caused even Oglethorpe to lose his temper and made him ill with fever.

Frequent afternoon showers seemed to multiply the insects beyond endurance, and the night guards' hands and faces and necks stayed swollen from bites. Only great bonfires brought relief, and fire intensified the heat—the summer was one long dreary cycle of heat, rain, and insects.

Still, nothing could discourage James for long. When he learned that his old friend Tomochichi was bringing a large party of Yamacraws to Frederica, he ordered a celebration fit for a distinguished member of the family. He ran down the steep river bank to greet the

Mico's periagua and proudly gave him a conducted tour of the new town.

"I and my chiefs can see with our eyes what you have accomplished in a very short time," Tomochichi said warmly. "This is already an important outpost. Now we, together, will stake out our common boundaries. Then we will rest and with bow and arrow hunt until the moon is new."

The Indians were as eager as the English to determine a line dividing their territory from the Spanish—a delicate matter which had already caused bloodshed —Yamacraws had recently been killed by Spanish soldiers at St. Augustine. Oglethorpe knew that Tomochichi was right, the next step was to explore the coastal area all the way south to the Spanish installations. Only then could they decide upon the most likely boundary. With the fortification of St. Simons, the line was already expanded south of what had been granted by the Crown. With total disregard for this and for Spain's previous claims, Oglethorpe envisioned English forts all the way to St. Augustine. The island immediately to the south he had named Jekyll on his first trip, the next one already had a Highlander lookout on it, so he referred to it as Highlands, but now he said to Toonahowi, "What shall we name it for our English maps?"

"I should like to honor the Duke of Cumberland who gave me the gold watch when I was in London," the boy said, lifting the treasure from a small pouch at his side.

"Excellent," Oglethorpe replied. "We will remember him at all times, as will the generations who follow us, Toonahowi." The lookout became Fort St. Andrew on Cumberland Island and on the extreme southern end, Fort William was built.

Santa Maria and San Juan islands were renamed Amelia and St. George. About halfway between St. George and Cumberland, the St. Johns River emptied into the Atlantic. The north bank should be a safe place to camp overnight, Oglethorpe decided. When Indian scouts reported back to him there, they told of seeing white men just across the St. Johns River.

"Let us attack them and revenge the deaths of our brothers," the head scout insisted.

"Without determining how many of them there are?" Oglethorpe said scornfully. "We will wait until morning and identify them if possible."

Even the scouts were grateful for his caution when the white campers across the St. Johns turned out to be, not Spaniards, but an Englishman—Major Richards and his crew.

"How do you happen to be in this godforsaken place?" James asked the Major. "The last I knew you were in Savannah."

"I was sent with Commissioner Dempsey, as you suggested, sir, to St. Augustine. He was hoping to arrange a convention between you and the Spanish Governor to discuss boundaries, but a squall caught us on the way. We had to swim for our lives. Fortunately, the Spanish found us on the beach."

"Did they treat you well?" Oglethorpe questioned.

"Yes, they were very polite. So was the Governor, Don Francisco del Morale Sanchez. We were taken to him at the St. Augustine *castillo*. He is also the military commander there."

"Would he discuss the boundary, Major?"

"Very little, really. But he gave me a letter to deliver to you." Richards took a roll of parchment from a bag and handed it to Oglethorpe. "He expects a reply within three weeks," he said.

Major Richards and his men started northward to

Savannah, leaving Oglethorpe to study the Spaniard's letter. Sanchez gave the impression that he wanted peaceful relations above all else. Having learned of Oglethorpe's influence over the Indians, he asked him to keep them from fighting in Spanish Florida.

"This man may be sincere," Oglethorpe mused, after reading the letter aloud to Tomochichi. "Or he may be trying to mislead me. What is your opinion?"

"I can only say that there is word that he has been stocking supplies of guns and powder," Tomochichi answered.

"Be that as it may, my friend, I want you to keep your men north of this river. They are to keep me informed of any forces crossing the St. Johns from Florida."

Sanchez's letter had aroused fresh suspicion. When Oglethorpe returned to his home, he ordered his men to build another fort—Fort St. Simons on the south end of the island. If an attack came, this fortification commanded the strategic Sound. Nevertheless, he wrote del Morale Sanchez that he, too, wanted peace.

Several months later, the Spanish Governor sent his secretary to Frederica. Not wanting a potential enemy to see the settlement or its defenses, Oglethorpe received the Spanish delegation on board a ship anchored in the Sound and manned by the burliest Scots he could find in Darien. The fierce-looking giants in colorful plaids carried their most impressive weapons —leather targes (shields) and in addition to their broadswords, vicious curved knives which they wore unsheathed.

Oglethorpe always liked to tell about the meeting that night with the Spanish emissary. As he toasted the King of Spain, Philip V, the ship's cannon were fired. Answering were cannon from the fort at Frederica, from

Fort St. Andrew, from Fort William—from all directions. "The Spanish were plainly surprised and confused," Oglethorpe chuckled. "You see, they hadn't even known those forts were there."

Undoubtedly the trickery strengthened the British position in the treaty which followed: Border disputes were to be peacefully settled by the English and Spanish Courts. That was about all it specified, and in the official circles back in Madrid, it was not considered enough. Sanchez should have been more aggressive. The least he should have done was order the British north, back to their old Altamaha border. For his peaceful efforts, the Spanish Governor was recalled to Spain in disgrace.

There was no doubt in Oglethorpe's mind what this meant—war.

Chapter 15

OGLETHORPE'S FEVERISH PREPARATIONS for hostilities with Spain did not equip him to deal with petty battles on the home front among the settlers. Upon leaving for Savannah one weekend, he gave an order that no one was to fire a gun on Sunday. But right in the middle of the Sabbath sermon, the quiet congregation was startled by a loud explosion. The constable ran out from the service to find Dr. Hawkins with a musket in his hands, a wild turkey slung over his shoulder. When the doctor was told to march to the commanding officer at the fort, he refused and it took the constable and two soldiers to get him there. When Oglethorpe came home, the doctor was still locked up and Frederica was afire with gossip. Gossip is inevitable in any community, but the smaller the town, the faster it spreads. To Oglethorpe's horror, some of it was being traced to Charles Wesley. James had been a friend of the Wesley family long before he asked Susannah Wesley, their mother, if the brothers could accompany him to Georgia. She had urged her sons to accept the great opportunity of preaching the Gospel to the heathen. Because Oglethorpe had been so lax in keeping the Trustees up to date on colony affairs, they had suggested this could be solved if Charles Wesley took care of such reports and acted as Oglethorpe's secretary. The Reverend John Wesley could do the preaching. John made Savannah his headquarters. Charles lived at Frederica.

At first, Charles Wesley and Oglethorpe worked well together, but it was not long before they were getting on each other's nerves and unconsciously competing for the colonists' loyalty. Charles complained that it was beneath him to do little more than take dictation day after day. For his part, Oglethorpe was getting tired of the people coming to him protesting Charles's holier-than-thou attitudes and his tactless attempts at reforming them. "He forces us to prayers, sir—and we don't like it!"

Worse than that, Charles Wesley was supposed to have hinted that Dr. Hawkins' wife had secretly seduced Oglethorpe. (Mrs. Hawkins went to such lengths to get attention, it's quite possible that she started the rumor herself.) Beatre Hawkins promptly accused Wesley of having taken unto himself "undue authority when he commanded that my husband be imprisoned." No wonder Oglethorpe was confused when he listened to all of the reasons Dr. Hawkins was under arrest. All he knew for certain was that the townsfolk were at one another's throats—some blaming Mrs. Hawkins, some, Charles Wesley.

"Send Wesley over to my house after dinner today," Oglethorpe told an orderly. The meeting was a stormy one. Oglethorpe completely lost his temper after getting nowhere in his attempt to clarify what had happened to cause such an uproar. Banging the desk between himself and his secretary, he shouted, "Finally, I accuse you, you puking adolescent, of mutiny and sedition! It has been called to my attention that you have been trying to persuade some of my men to desert this colony. Is that true?"

"How can you believe such a thing, sir?" Charles asked weakly. "You know my heart is incapable of such betrayal."

"I know no such thing. Your infernal meddling is directly responsible for the death of that baby born Sunday night. You jailed the doctor! He could not attend the mother. You are not only working behind my back to overthrow my authority, you are a murderer!"

"Stop, sir," Charles pleaded. "You are saying things you cannot mean. I flatly deny that I had anything whatever to do with Dr. Hawkins' imprisonment. The good doctor's wife is using you, sir. Ever since I prayed for her sins in public meeting, she has tried to turn you against me. Now you are charging me with all of that she-devil's mischief."

"The evidence charges you, Mr. Wesley," James snapped. "It is the more serious when I see no love, no meekness, no true religion, but must endure mere formal prayers from you. Your misdirected zeal is a poor substitute for true piety! Now, will you do me the great favor of leaving!"

From that time on, Wesley was increasingly peevish and miserable. People looked the other way when they met him. The woman who had always laundered his linen sent it back unwashed. Even the board on which he slept was taken away on the orders of Oglethorpe. In desperation, Charles sent for older brother John, who came at once from Savannah.

Had John been an objective arbiter, he might have made both men admit they were behaving like children over the most insignificant issues. Then he could have brought about a reconciliation. Instead, he acted as though there was no quarrel and made no attempt to determine the facts. In a few days he went back to Savannah, having done nothing more than preach a few sermons on the theme "Judge not."

Contrary to some versions of the estrangement between Oglethorpe and Charles Wesley, the story had a happy ending, which simply proves that they were both not only vain men but dramatic men as well.

Every rumor that the Spanish were coming north sent James off on a scouting mission, and each time he was certain he would never return. One day when such an alarm reached him at Frederica, he sent for his secretary, who must have been startled. "You know what has passed between us, Wesley, but I am now going to my death. You will see me no more. Take this ring and deliver it to Trustee Vernon in London. He will look after you and your brother. I have intercepted letters saying the Spaniards intend to cut us off at a blow. But death is to me nothing. I go to it now."

Overcome with remorse and concern, Charles Wesley cried, "We were both deceived by mischief-makers!

I want you to go away knowing in your heart I am innocent of the charges against me, sir."

"Of course, you are innocent, Wesley. My old confidence in you is what you must remember," Oglethorpe said. "I embrace and kiss you in farewell, and with the most cordial affection."

The instant reconciliation was almost more than Charles could believe, but Oglethorpe meant it, inviting Charles to accompany him to his waiting scout boat where an officer presented him his sword. "Wesley, with this my beloved father's sword, I was never before unsuccessful."

"I hope, sir, you carry with you a better one," Charles said fervently. "Even the sword of the Lord and of Gideon."

"I hope so, too!" Oglethorpe's boat shoved off as he called buoyantly to the Frederica folk clustered on the shore, "God bless you all!"

Oglethorpe did return, and by the time Charles resigned to leave for home, thanks to James, he was also restored to the good graces of the Frederica settlers.

Chapter 16

TWO MONTHS LATER, the Trustees requested that James attend the January session of Parliament, which was in no mood to grant further support for Georgia. Once more Oglethorpe's judgment in the handling of money was in question. Serious misunderstandings were sprouting within South Carolina over Georgia's prohibition of rum. The Carolinians were smuggling it south in startling quantity—feeling they had a right to any such profits. After all, hadn't their financial aid helped the infant colony get started? Besides, their monopoly of Indian trade was being wiped out by Georgia's competition. As Oglethorpe's prestige with the Indians had grown, Carolina's had shriveled.

Men who welcomed James to America as a hero now turned against him, furtively sending reports to London which claimed that he was exceeding his authority —that he had secretly trafficked in furs for personal profit; that he was turning the French against Carolina.

For the first time, Oglethorpe's administration of Georgia was censured. He departed in a storm of charges and countercharges almost as violent as the ocean that buffeted his ship en route to England that January. Day after day, navigation was impossible because of fog. The helpless ship was finally hurled into the breakers near a strange coast. The terrified crewmen deserted their posts and Oglethorpe, along with other passengers, jumped out of bed in their nightshirts to save the ship from going aground. It was not until they were safe in Wales that James admitted, "That was the narrowest escape of my life!"

Soon after his arrival in England, Oglethorpe attended a four-hour conference with the Trustees of the Georgia Colony. He was ready for them, defending his colony with great charm and skill. He even convinced his associates that the Georgia funds had been used efficiently, emphasizing the value of the (unauthorized) fortifications on St. Simons in his effort to maintain peace with the Spanish. By the time he had finished his report, the Trustees again voted him their confidence and thanks.

When at last the Carolina charges came up, opinion was once more on Oglethorpe's side, and when he countered with facts about the Carolinians' rum-running and illicit trade with Indians outside their territory, a compromise was ordered. The Carolinians must deal with licensed traders only, just as the Georgians did.

James knew that it would be much tougher to justify his military penetration south of the Altamaha River. The English Secretary of State, Thomas Newcastle, had already received numerous complaints about it from Don Tomas Geraldino, the Spanish representative in London. Evading a stand, Newcastle passed responsibility to the Trustees, who in turn blandly said the subjects of the King of Spain in Florida had not been molested. "We are sure that reports of established defenses in Spanish territory are without foundation," the Trustees said.

When he met Don Tomas Geraldino face to face, Oglethorpe claimed that his intentions had all been clearly spelled out in the treaty made earlier with del Morale Sanchez. But Geraldino did not believe Oglethorpe, nor did Spain consider the treaty valid. Consequently, an immediate reinforcement of St. Augustine was ordered.

This strengthened Oglethorpe's request for 30,000 pounds to defend Georgia, but it was not until March that the slow-moving Government gave him the funds, granted him a regiment of seven hundred men and commissioned him General of the Forces of South Carolina and Georgia. At last, he would be able to form a militia to defend the colony against the Spanish and the French.

Reports on battle preparations in Cuba and St.

Augustine reached Charles Town finally, reminding Carolina that Georgia was the only buffer between it and the enemy. The tide which had so recently turned against Oglethorpe in America was quickly reversed.

Recognizing the power the General now commanded, Don Tomas Geraldino's next move was to ask Prime Minister Sir Robert Walpole to detain Oglethorpe in England. Walpole refused. The Spanish diplomat interpreted this to mean the British Government could no longer restrain their commander and Geraldino countered with threats of reprisals.

Walpole knew the situation could easily turn into open conflict. In his anxiety, he canceled the grant of money for the colonial militia and sent for Oglethorpe, who was shocked when the Prime Minister said, "I must ask you to disband your regiment of regular forces, General. It is the only way my government can prove its peaceful intentions toward Spain."

"What kind of man do you take me to be?" Oglethorpe responded, his voice icy and sarcastic. "Do you think I have no conscience? I took the responsibility of leading hundreds of souls to Georgia to live in safety and prosperity. Are you asking me to abandon them to be murdered by the Spanish, sir? I will not be your pawn!"

Whether the General's logic or his favoritism with the King influenced Walpole, the Prime Minister reversed himself again. The following September, 1737, Oglethorpe recruited his regiment straight from the King's own choice infantry, the Twenty-fifth Foot. Only forty years old, James was now one of the most important military figures in the American colonies.

Part Three

1737 – 1743

Chapter 17

JUST BEFORE THE General left for Georgia, the Trustees plainly warned him that he was to supervise the defenses of the Georgia-Carolina territory but all civil administration must be left to them. This was humiliating enough, but in a final audience with George II, the King said, as though instructing an impulsive youth, "Avoid giving any just cause of offence or jealousy to the Spaniards. As my representative, you are expected to maintain the strictest friendship."

When James marched his new regiment onto the shores of St. Simons several weeks later, his administrative authority had eroded away, but he *was* the military commander. The islanders greeted the troops with relief and their general with "extreme delight." On a whirlwind trip to Charles Town and Savannah, he was welcomed with ceremony, but the warmest reception of all came from Tomochichi and his people. One thing at least had not changed—Oglethorpe's bond with the Indians was as strong as ever.

He found Tomochichi thin and drawn from a long serious illness. When he looked into his friend's face, the aged Indian straightened his bent shoulders and said, "Seeing the Great Man again restores me, makes me feel as lofty as an eagle." Accompanied by a group of chiefs, Tomochichi explained why so many Indians had gathered to greet Oglethorpe in Savannah, "The Spanish have spread the word that you are in St. Augustine. My people know you cannot be in two places at once. They are here to see you for themselves."

"Why would they tell such an obvious lie?" Oglethorpe wondered.

"To trap our best men," Tomochichi answered. "Our delegation was suspicious from the beginning, but they went to St. Augustine in case you were there and needed them. When they asked for you, they were told you lay ill on a ship in the harbor. Then the Spaniards showered them with valuable gifts and tried to bribe them to break with the English."

Instead of falling into the trap of the wily Spanish, the Indians returned to Savannah to wait "The Great Man's" coming. Now they pledged their allegiance to him yet again. He had never needed them more. He would enlist them in a strategy of defense that would deter the French on the west, the Spanish to the south. Some he would assign to the forts he planned all along the length of the inland waterway. Some would range the woods reconnoitering. Some would be trained for sudden expeditions with the troops.

"I am too old to be more than your advisor," Tomochichi said wistfully. "But these men are ready to serve you at any time against the common enemy. One thousand Creeks are prepared to march anywhere you command them."

It was not the first time Oglethorpe felt that the red men were more loyal to him than were his own countrymen. When he was invited to visit Indian towns, some of them as far away as four hundred miles, he recognized the honor and promised to make the journey. He

90

also wrote the Trustees that in light of all the trouble the Spanish were stirring up with their bribes and illegal trading, he must attend a meeting of all the Creek leaders in Coweta town. "I must support the honest natives or they will be overcome," he wrote. "In that case the whole Creek nation will be forced into war against England."

Coweta lay many miles to the west. If any white men could survive the expedition, Oglethorpe decided the Darien Highlanders were his best choice. Officers Dunbar, Leman, and Eyre were about the most fearless, untiring white men he knew, and they had maintained close ties with the Indians. Accompanied by them, the General took a cutter up the Savannah River twenty-five miles above Ebenezer to Uchee town. There, Indian traders met the party with horses needed for the rest of the journey. "We are your volunteer guides to Coweta," the Indians announced.

The travelers slowly worked their way through the wilderness, day after day wading swamps, hacking through thickets, forging strange rivers. When they stopped for sleep, Oglethorpe, wrapped only in his cloak, lay on the hard ground beside the Indians. For two hundred miles they did not meet a living soul, then they came upon a worn trail where they found baskets of food left for them by local red men. Forty miles from Coweta, the party was met by a delegation of chiefs who escorted Oglethorpe to their meeting place.

The council opened with solemn rites and eloquent tributes to "The Great Man who has undertaken the long journey unafraid, attended by few white men, showing faith in us and accommodating himself to our habits. By the natural dignity of his deportment, he

91

wins the hearts of his red brothers whom he has never deceived."

For several days, James Oglethorpe talked earnestly with the Creeks, smoked the hallowed pipes of peace, watched their ritual dances, even sipped small quantities of the black drink, *foskey,* offered only to their "Beloved Men" as a special honor. *Foskey,* made from the leaves and young shoots of cassina, was prepared with much formality, a sacred concoction for the chosen. It was described as "most exhilarating," and it is worth noting that the white General could partake sparingly of it through ten long days of conference and still arrive at a lucid, reasonable treaty. The treaty confirmed previous grants of territory and renewed Creek loyalty to the English Crown which promised the Indians fair trade. In addition, Oglethorpe persuaded the Creeks to refrain from killing those traders who had abused them and talked the Choctaws out of warring against the French who threatened their western frontier. If the French, as rumored, succeeded in marching south from Quebec and east from the Mississippi, allied with Indians in their pay, the Creeks were the only hope the Carolinians had. The Creeks were the key defense.

No wonder the Trustees wrote in response to Oglethorpe's detailed report on the treaty: "The Carolina people, as well as everyone else, must own that no one ever engaged the Indians so strongly in affection as yourself."

The treaty was essential for the basic peace of Georgia, but so was the journey itself. Long afterward, men and boys talked about the General's endurance and courage. After all, the Spanish would have paid a fortune for his head. Just one treacherous Indian out of the thousands in Coweta could have murdered him there or on the lonely trail. The hardships of the trip and exhaustion from the endless discussions took their toll—James became ill. Fortunately, he was near Fort Augusta and was able to rest there until his fever subsided.

When he arrived in Savannah, still weak, he was faced at once with emergencies. The Spanish had been agitating rebellion among Carolina slaves, promising them protection and presents if they would run away to Florida. Planter-owners demanded that Oglethorpe get their "property" back from the Florida Governor. James tried, and although the response was friendly, it was negative.

Suspecting the Spanish of luring the slaves south in order to force them into military service, he sent rangers and Indian runners in pursuit of the black slaves, with orders to "Cut off their escape and bring them back to their owners." Then he called a public meeting at the Savannah courthouse to calm the fears of the people there and said, "I have taken precautions to prevent a surprise attack from the west or the south, a convoy of English frigates is cruising the coast at this moment, and I expect reinforcements for our land troops. Carolina and Georgia will be protected. I give you my word."

Oglethorpe did more than assure the citizens of their safety. He gave them something to do: "I observe that the Common and city squares are overgrown with weeds and brush from long neglect. Lazy citizens are seldom safe citizens. Let's clean up Savannah!"

With great and small problems plaguing him, James, busier than ever and more irritable, was unprepared for the sudden grief that struck him. Tomochichi, his beloved, faithful friend, died ... "full of years, conquered only by time."

The old Indian king's last words were for his white brother. As Senauki and Toonahowi sat on either side fanning the dying chief, Tomochichi, propped against the trunk of a live oak, exhorted his kinsmen, "Do not forget ever the kindness of The Great Man Oglethorpe, nor the benefits he has brought us from the English." Tomochichi's ancient eyes closed and he clasped his long, graceful hands prayerfully on his breast. "Because it was in Savannah that I first met and helped The Great Man, I want to be buried there with Christian ceremony."

The noble though wasted body was brought down the river from Yamacraw, and at the foot of Savannah bluff Oglethorpe received it. Contrary to Creek tradition, it was not bound to a stretcher of skins but lay on a bed of green pine boughs in a shallow coffin. The coffin was made of pine and scaly layers of bark remained on its outer sides. With four of Savannah's honorable magistrates, James Oglethorpe proudly carried the coffin to the central square of the town as its one bell tolled and uniformed young men beat a muffled tattoo on their drums.

The Indian mourners listened to the Christian scriptures and prayers without showing emotion, until the end of the service when James Edward Oglethorpe took his esteemed but lonely place at the head of Tomochichi's open grave. The General's head was bowed, his eyes closed, and tears fell unashamedly on his hand which gripped the handle of his sword. The Indians wept with The Great Man, and with him they were one in their sorrow.

I could not have founded this colony without Tomo-

94

chichi, James thought—Tomochichi, an Indian, mighty
and humble, was Georgia's real king.

Chapter 18

SINCE 1565, WHEN Pedro Menéndez de Avilés routed
the French to found St. Augustine, the Spanish had
considered southeastern America theirs. But they had
been forced to abandon Carolina to the British and had
gradually withdrawn to the northern border of the
Florida territory, leaving the area in between what his-
torians later called "The Debatable Land." Under-
standably, the Spanish resented the aggressive acts of
English smugglers who were crossing the Atlantic to
deliver prohibited goods to Spanish colonies. Aggressive, too, was Oglethorpe's construction of defenses
along the Georgia coast.

Smouldering hostility between the two great powers,
Spain and England, erupted incident after incident.
British merchants, flouting treaty agreements which re-
stricted their trade in Spanish ports, smuggled their
goods at an alarming rate into Florida, Cuba, and the
West Indies. Consequently, their ships were being
seized continuously by Spanish "coast guards" who
were known for their brutal tortures.

One victim of their revenge, Thomas Jenkins, particularly, fired the emotions of the members of Parliament when he described the raid on his ship. In the
struggle between the British crew and the Spanish sailors, a Latin sliced off Captain Jenkins' ear, waved it
under his nose shouting, "I only wish I could perform

the same atrocity upon the King of England!"

Captain Jenkins had carefully preserved the gory ear and at the proper moment in the telling of his story, held it high for all the gentlemen in Commons to see. The propaganda value would be hard to estimate. Instantly, every man in the room was ready to take up arms against the barbaric enemy. It mattered not one bit that the fifty-two vessels reportedly plundered belonged to lawbreaking smugglers like Jenkins.

Prime Minister Walpole felt the tide of opinion turn against him overnight. His concern was for England to have time and peace in which to develop world trade. War with Spain would seriously deter that development. To stall, to avoid action, he asked for a convention with Spain. The discussions boiled down to two issues: Reparations for the English shipping which Spain had destroyed and the disputed Georgia boundary. If Spain paid the reparations, would England withdraw her settlers and trade and defenses to the old Carolina line? That was the final question. Walpole did not want to give up Georgia, as he was later charged but, as he saw it, if that was the price of peace with his rival, Spain, he had no other choice.

In protest to this decision, some of the Georgia Trustees resigned. The Earl of Egmont, Colonel Bladen, Henry Towers, and Henry Archer defended the colony. Too much had gone into Georgia for it to be deserted for any reason, they argued, convincing the House of Commons that Walpole's policy should be opposed. Without a majority support, he could not negotiate further. The alternative was war.

One might say that popular opinion forced the Prime Minister to declare war on Spain. It became official, October 23, 1739, and Oglethorpe's moves against the enemy would be only a small part of the Crown's imperial struggle, known as King George's War, which would continue until 1748.

The Spanish made plans immediately to attack Georgia—by land, aided by Indians and slaves; by water, hoping to wipe out regular troops stationed at English forts along the coast. They knew Oglethorpe would be ordered to protect the colony. He must be driven out once and for all.

It was at this critical time that a number of troops the General had brought from Gibraltar marched on his tent and demanded "full subsistence and back pay." The government funds to support these additional men had not arrived, nor had the support he had requested from Carolina. With care, he explained his position to the angry men.

"I regret there is nothing I can do to meet your demands at this time," he said. "I hope to do so in the near future. Now, will you return to your quarters in good order."

As the General turned to reenter his tent, two shots rang out, both meant for him. One was a wide miss, the other singed his cheek and wig. His guards rushed the would-be assassin and killed him on the spot. The mutiny petered out when its leaders were promptly court-martialed, and the dead rebel was hanged from a tree limb for all to see. When the uprising was reported in Parliament, even the Trustees who had failed to back Oglethorpe were relieved that he had not been murdered. He was the only one, after all, who could lead the defense of the southern border.

His orders were to harass the enemy forces. This could best be done, he decided, with a surprise expedition against St. Augustine before the Spanish were fully prepared to resist. Intelligence indicated a shortage of provisions there. Also, the galleys that normally guarded the harbor had been sent to Havana for reinforcements. That alone improved Oglethorpe's chances of overwhelming the Augustine stronghold. By express messenger, he begged his friend, Governor Bull, for support. Bull put the request before the Carolina Assembly, recommending that a regiment be raised. Including Virginians, it would total six hundred men under the command of Colonel Vander Dussen, four ships, two sloops, and 120,000 pounds. While these decisions were made by the assembly, little was done about them. The French, through Indians friendly to them, were now stepping up their pressure against Carolina. Was it safe to divide Carolina's forces by sending aid to Oglethorpe in the south so far away?

The Carolinians' delay added to the General's frustration at not receiving from England the money, arms, and horses he needed. Even his warning was ignored: "If we don't take St. Augustine, there is nothing to stop the enemy short of Virginia." Finally, James went to plead in person before the Carolina Assembly and again was promised aid.

Instead of six hundred troops, twenty showed up; instead of the one thousand Indians expected, there were one hundred. In spited of this, with the four hundred men of his own regiment, a company of Darien Highlanders, several units of Indians (Toonahowi now led the Yamacraws), cavalry, and foot soldiers raised from all sections of Georgia, General Oglethorpe assembled his motley forces at the mouth of the St. Johns River.

With a carefully selected company, he pushed on to a small Spanish fort, Diego, twenty-five miles from St.

98

Augustine. On the way, the English were attacked by hostile Indians in the service of the enemy. Though the ambush was repulsed, the soldier leading Oglethorpe's horse was killed. Spurred by the incident, the English charged Diego and took it. The General had gained a strategic base in enemy territory and prisoners from whom he could learn the enemy's plans.

Sixty men under Captain Dunbar were left to garrison Diego while the General returned to the St. Johns River encampment where the Carolinians were expected. Vander Dussen arrived at last with the full Carolina regiment. Captain John McIntosh Mor with a Darien company of Highland Rangers joined them. The reinforcements encouraged Oglethorpe just as he received the alarming news that six Spanish warships with long brass nine-pounder cannon and two sloops of provisions had reached St. Augustine. The town was suddenly supplied with fresh troops, arms, and food. This was a blow Oglethorpe had not expected. He dared not wait any longer. With his combined forces he must advance at once on St. Augustine.

The town had been founded in 1565 by Pedro Menéndez de Avilés, near the place where Ponce de Léon landed fifty-two years earlier. Sir Frances Drake, Queen Elizabeth's famous buccaneer, burned it down in 1586. In 1702, the British attacked it again. St. Augustine had reason to protect itself with a fort large enough to hold all of its population.

The fort Castillo de San Marcos was built from coquina stone brought from Anastasia Island just across the harbor. Cannonballs were said literally to bounce off this unique shell material. If that was an exaggeration, it was still unlikely that any ammunition could penetrate the *castillo's* walls. They were twelve feet thick and thirty feet high. At each corner of its square design was a bastion—on each bastion a watchtower. Connecting the towers was a parapet with openings through which fifty cannon pointed, guarding all approaches. Only two years before, the *castillo* had been reinforced to take any British attack. Around it the deep moat was kept filled with water. Beyond the moat lay the town, and around the town, a newly repaired wall. Behind it, waited a garrison of "700 regulars, 2 troops of horse, 4 companies of armed blacks, the militia of the province and Indians." Governor Montiano did not wait for Oglethorpe unprepared.

The banners which flew above the Castillo de San Marcos snapped defiance.

Upon orders from the Royal Admiralty, Commodore Vincent Pearse, aboard the flatship *Flamborough,* planned to aid Oglethorpe by leading his armed fleet of seven in an attack from the harbor side. But when Pearse and his armada approached the inlet, there were the Spanish warships just returned from Cuba, their formidable guns sweeping all sea approaches to the *castillo.* Pearse was helpless short of open engagement. Oglethorpe would have to try the land assault alone, without the promised naval bombardment from the ships. He knew he could not do it. Now the plan to storm the castle-fort must be abandoned.

Still, he reasoned he could set up a blockade. His first move was invasion of the island of Anastasia opposite the *castillo,* driving the Spanish forces stationed there to the mainland. With Vander Dussen's battery on a nearby point of land and Pearse's cannon off shore, Oglethorpe decided, their fire combined with his on the island would terrify the people of St. Augustine—they would flee inside the *castillo* for safety. Once this happened, he could count on the additional demand for supplies and the mounting chaos which would force Montiano to surrender. The Spanish themselves would turn the siege into an English victory.

Instead of the chaos imagined by Oglethorpe, the *castillo* was prepared, orderly, its defenders equalled the number of attackers, its artillery heavier and better concentrated. More than that, Montiano was spoiling for a fight. Montiano was confident.

When the English General sent a message to the Spanish Governor demanding surrender, Montiano replied, "I shall be happy to shake your hand if you will meet me inside the *castillo.*" Such a cocky response should have been a warning, but Oglethorpe gave the command to open fire on St. Augustine and its fortress. His eighteen-pound cannon were answered by those atop the *castillo.* The one thousand yards that separated them kept either side from hurting the other—the bombardment was about as damaging as bowling on the green.

Stationed in wooded areas north of the town were the Highland Rangers and Indian warriors. Once the fort was penetrated, their orders were to move in and help force a final surrender. Meanwhile, they were to keep moving, ranging the countryside, preventing any supplies or troops from getting through. Pearse would intercept any reinforcements arriving by way of the sea. But in no time at all, both the Rangers and the sailors were trapped—the Rangers by Spaniards who surrounded them in an old log fort and slaughtered half of them; the sailors by a threatening hurricane. Pearse, "whose discretion was more conspicuous than his valour," decided the fleet was in danger and moved it out of the battle zone. Even the Indians, by now convinced there was going to be little hand-to-hand fighting, saw no reason to stay, and many of the Carolinians joined them on their homeward trek. There simply was no significant action. Why wait and wait for something to happen while mosquitoes and sandflies tortured them into madness? They preferred being casualties of battle. Fourteen had died of fever, but not one had been killed by the enemy.

Oglethorpe, stranded with only Georgia troops who were bone-tired from tropical heat and rain, insects and boredom, turned more desperate than daring—his hopes of assaulting the *castillo* and capturing St. Augustine faded in the July sun.

Retreat was the only course open to him. He ordered the artillery and provisions on Anastasia removed to the mainland. Vander Dussen marched his remaining men back to the St. Johns River base camp. Aware that the English General was left with limited support, the Spanish sent out five hundred men to attack him. Outnumbered but fearless, the English repulsed the enemy, drove them inside the town entrenchments, and for Oglethorpe, this was the only triumphant moment in the thirty-eight-day siege! "With drums beating and colors flying," he led his troops away as though they had just concluded a victorious campaign.

Chapter 19

BY THE TIME James reached his home at Frederica, he was depressed, once more weakened and ill with fever.

But he wrote the Trustees that he would not abandon Georgia. Though the siege on St. Augustine seemed a failure, he was certain that it would at least deter the Spanish for a time. He must train his troops better. It would be costly, as the Florida campaign had been costly. Could the Trustees send money at once so that he might prepare for the invasion that was bound to come?

In London, Thomas Stephens, an agitator from Savannah, who had been giving wild reports on the affairs of Georgia, used the recent military setback to bolster charges of Oglethorpe's incompetence just when the General most needed a united colony to stand with him.

Stephens had been sent to London by a group of malcontents. He claimed to speak as a representative of 121 Savannahians. Already they had signed a petition demanding that the Trustees grant them the right to buy rum and slaves. They also wanted absolute ownership of land. They claimed that the population of Georgia was dwindling, that the colony was "in a starving and despicable condition." They reported fictitious Spanish victories which comforted the enemy. This was not all: Carolina pamphleteers were equally busy discrediting the Trustees and Oglethorpe. He was described "guilty of cowardice, despotism, cruelty and bribery." His stand against rum and slavery was called an "obstruction."

Small wonder that James repeatedly took to his bed with "fatigue and vexation." And the worst was yet to come. France linked her naval strength with Spain's against the British, and war broke out once more in Europe. To the Crown, Georgia was suddenly insignificant compared with such a tremendous continental involvement. There were now no resources that could be spared for the American colonies.

Turning once more to Carolina for help, Oglethorpe cited his intelligence reports about Spanish forces from Cuba and Florida which were readying an attack upon St. Simons Island. The Carolina Assembly, like Parliament, did nothing. This time even Governor Bull failed to respond to his old friend's plea.

A lesser man would have taken the next ship home. Instead, still certain that the Spanish could be bested in actual battle, the General began strengthening all of the fortifications along the Georgia coast, especially those on St. Simons. To the Trustees he wrote, "I think we are more likely to succeed in this place than we were before we knew our opposition." He may have been inwardly discouraged, but he was not afraid, and he was not going to quit.

From a village of palmetto-thatched huts, Frederica had grown into a self-sustaining, prosperous town. Events now reminded its citizens why it had been established as a military outpost. Under Oglethorpe's driving supervision, parallel palisades were completed to encircle the town. The fort and the King's magazine were secured. The earthworks heightened. Extra cannon were strung along the banks which could direct a line of fire up or down the river. Fort St. Simons on the southern tip of the island was also readied for attack, and roads were completed between lookouts. Four years before, Oglethorpe had built a military road which wound north along the edge of the eastern marshes, connecting Fort St. Simons with Frederica.

An intercepted message justified the General's preparations. The message revealed that Montiano's superiors in Cuba had instructed him to proceed up the inland waterway, plunder and burn all settlements and forts between St. Augustine and Carolina's Port Royal. Oglethorpe read the message without surprise. "Montiano will head straight for St. Simons," he predicted. "This is the strongest defense he'll have to get past. We will see to it that he does not. That is the only way we can make sure he does not reach Savannah nor Port Royal."

Messages were posted to the Creek allies, to Captain Hugh Mackay and his Darien Highlanders, to Captain Carr and his company of marines, to the rangers and engineers of Carolina. Captain Dunbar was dispatched to Fort William, Captain Horton to Fort Andrew, but after brief skirmishes with the Spanish, these two officers brought their men to reinforce Fort Frederica.

On the 28th of June, 1742, a lookout at Fort St. Simons spotted a fleet of over thirty ships sailing up the coast. As they came nearer, he could identify the red and white flag of Spain. He knew they were heading straight for St. Simons. He must send a messenger to Frederica with the news.

"Enemy sail sighted, sir," an out-of-breath boy reported when he was brought before Oglethorpe.

"Do you know how many?"

"I counted thirty, sir, but there are more in the distance.

Turning to his aide, the General spoke calmly, "See that every available horse is mounted by a man capable of patroling our island's beaches. Pass the word that extra duty will be required. Those acquitting themselves in distinguished ways will be advanced, and take care not to alarm the townspeople unduly." He knew he must keep up the spirits of the people, and get word to

Bull that the enemy was at hand. I can no longer be accused of false alarms or imagined danger, he mused. The enemy is here!

For a week, the Spanish anchored to the south, sounding the depth of the channel, studying the tides and wind. On July 5, they moved in on the flood tide.

The batteries of Fort St. Simons and the defending British ships opened fire on the Spanish ships with unexpected power and timing. When a 22-gun enemy ship came alongside the H.M.S. *Success* to put Spanish sailors aboard, it was turned back. The engagement between the Spaniards and Captain Carr's marines and Lieutenant Wall's infantry lasted nearly three hours. Both sides took casualties, the enemy the most—seventeen killed, ten wounded.

This did not keep the Spanish from moving on up the river beyond Fort St. Simons where they landed not far from Captain Gascoigne's shipyard. Here they set up a battery of twenty guns out of reach of English fire. The Spanish were now in a position to spread out their regiment and capture Fort St. Simons from the rear. Oglethorpe knew this would be disastrous so he resolutely ordered the fort abandoned by the six companies defending it.

"Bring everything that we can use to Frederica," he commanded. "Destroy what you must leave behind. Dismantle the fort, spike the cannon, ruin the wells. We will not surrender a gun nor leave them a drink of water!" Fresh water was most important to the Spaniards. They had guns.

Scouting parties of Indians and rangers were sent in all directions to spy on the invaders. The reports estimated that the enemy numbered almost five thousand men, but they were a poorly disciplined assortment of

106

irregulars. Not knowing exactly where Fort Frederica was located on the island, Montiano risked sending out parties in search of it. Unaccustomed to semijungle terrain, these soldiers hacked their way though dense thickets of palmetto, scrub oak, and vines where the English rangers and their Indians lurked, ready to pounce upon, to harass, to confuse the enemy. Every move of the Spanish was reported to Oglethorpe who, praying for time, expected reinforcements from Carolina to arrive at any moment. His little army of seven hundred was so outnumbered, and his provisions so limited, he needed those men from the neighbor colony more than ever before.

Montiano was not waiting for the Carolinians. At nine o'clock on the morning of July 7, a ranger brought word to Frederica that some two hundred of the enemy had discovered the Military Road (in most places it was a narrow path) leading from the south end of St. Simons Island north to Frederica, and, at that moment, an advance party was reconnoitering the area only two miles away.

The English, drilled to a peak of readiness, rushed after the General as he leaped on his favorite mount and with sword whipping the air around his head, charged out from the fort, down the road to meet the enemy. Toonahowi and the Yamacraws streaked after, their war paint glistening on their dark skins in the morning sun. When he came close to where the Spanish were, Oglethorpe took advantage of his own familiarity with the dense woods and stationed his men behind trees hoping to sneak up on the Spaniards. But with the sound of the first musket blast, men on both sides sprang from their hiding places to grapple hand-to-hand.

Oglethorpe himself fought off two charging enemy soldiers at sword's point and forced them to surrender. Toonahowi, shot in the right arm, managed to prime his pistol with his left hand and fire back at his assailant whom he instantly killed. Captain Sachio, leader of the Spanish party, found himself the prisoner of Lieutenant Scroggs and begged for mercy. The English fought fiercely, in good order, and drove back the Latins a step at a time until they withdrew from the bloody combat.

Chapter 20

OGLETHORPE REALIZED THAT the pause in the fighting could not last. If the Spanish regrouped and came again to this same spot on Military Road, which was logical, he knew they must be decisively repulsed or they would overrun his limited forces and take Fort Frederica. Gathering his officers around him, he plotted an ambush. The fearless Highlanders he dispatched into the dark tangle of woods which grew close to the right edge of a long curve in the Military Road. On the left was a salt marsh stretching off to the sea. At this point, the road was scarcely wide enough for two men abreast to pass. Cannon of any size could not get through. Oglethorpe had planned the road that way.

One question after another tumbled through his mind. What if I am miscalculating? What if the Spanish do not try to come up Military Road again? What if they are scheming to pin me down, away from the fort, while their boats steal up the river to capture Frederica? The General wheeled his horse about and raced back to Fort Frederica. He must warn the rangers and boatmen patrolling the shore there to be prepared in case the enemy approached from the south around the bend of the river. He must also calm and reassure the women and children. Both tasks he must handle in person.

What Oglethorpe did not know was that while he was organizing Frederica's defenses, three Spanish captains were leading one hundred grenadiers and two hundred foot soldiers, with Indians and Negroes, up the very road he had just left. Sure now that their superior numbers could easily overpower the English, the Spaniards boldly marched to drums, cheering loudly as they advanced. They were here to fight—to win. There was no longer any need to be secretive.

Directly south of the narrowest squeeze in Military Road was a savannah, a flat and open area, unprotected by trees. Here the enemy stopped, stacked their arms, scattered, and began building fires. It was dinnertime, they would eat. Any soldier fights better on a full stomach.

Not more than one hundred paces away, Oglethorpe's Indians and Scots watched, hidden in the underbrush. Though their General was back at Frederica, they knew well what to do. At the right moment they would leap out from ambush and murder the Spanish at their cooking pots.

Like rippling shadows, Toonahowi's men passed from tree to tree, moving nearer the edge of the woods. The Highlanders, as much at home in the forests as their "native" friends, crawled steadily forward. Unaware and off-guard, the Latins laughed and joked, hearing nothing. But one of their horses either heard a sound or glimpsed a sudden shaft of light off the highly polished shield of an approaching Scot. The animal whinnied and reared.

Automatically, the Spaniards grabbed muskets, whipped out pistols, and tried to assemble into a line of battle. The British, trained in the guerrillalike tactics of the Indians, rushed whooping from all directions, firing point-blank into the mass of enemy troops. The attack was at such close range, the Indians could send their tomahawks straight at faces and necks unprotected by heavy Spanish armor, while the giant Scots plunged bayonets and dirks into every full belly they could catch. With bagpipes skirling the Charge, Highlanders and Indians shrieked and yelled, dancing from one trapped enemy to another. At first the Spanish were horrified, shocked out of their wits, then they began fighting back. They fired at random into the woods, striking more trees than Englishmen, but held their ground for a time.

Oglethorpe, at Frederica, heard the barrage of gunfire, left the fort and once more streaked down Military Road to rejoin his regiment. The sun which had been blinding moments before was now hidden by a gray cloud moving rapidly out of the southwest, sending before it gusts of wind and a spatter of rain. The shower combined with a dense fog of powder smoke made it impossible for him to see his men until he was right on them, but he could tell they were falling back in disorder. "Return to the front, cowards," he shouted above the explosion and screams. "Do your duty by the paltry Latins! Shoot them! Kill them! Gut them! But move forward and find them! Move, I say!"

"We can't see to direct our fire, sir, and Lieutenant Sutherland has been killed," one soldier cried.

"Then follow me," the General bellowed.

Lieutenant Patrick Sutherland was one of his most valued officers—leader of the Highlanders—but this was not the time to stop and weigh the loss, not now. The General galloped into the thick of the combat to find his front line advancing rapidly again, routing an overwhelmed, straggling enemy rear guard. There, shouting orders, was Sutherland, very much alive.

Before the sudden rain had stopped, the Spanish retreated around the curve from which they had emerged so confidently a short time before, leaving behind their dead and wounded, their discarded weapons and half-emptied cooking pots. Unreliable reports of their casualties vary from two hundred to a thousand. That the slaughter was horrific is verified by the name since given it—the Battle of Bloody Marsh—which describes that fearful day and is still preserved on a bronze marker near the spot.

Oglethorpe now sent parties of Indians and rangers to harass the enemy and to report their movements. On the Frederica parade ground he reviewed his fatigued troops and rewarded the heroes of the battle with promotions. Lieutenant Sutherland was made a Brigade Major. The townsfolk were proud but weary spectators.

Addressing the citizens along with the soldiers, the General commended them for their "cheerful spirits" in the face of danger and warned, "The need for union and vigilance is not over. You must continue to give prompt attention to orders. You must maintain unflinching firmness in every emergency, for your safety, under God, depends on courage and readiness."

While he assured and praised his people, Oglethorpe concealed his own despair. Carolina was not going to help him, that was plain. With the enemy watching the harbor and river, no supplies could be brought in, and provisions were dwindling. Did Montiano know that? What would be Montiano's next move? It was unlikely he would send men up the Military Road again, and there was only one other thing he could do—come up the river.

On July 11, three Spanish ships were sighted rounding the bend to the south of Fort Frederica. Before they could maneuver into firing position, the British opened up with a bombardment Oglethorpe had readied four days earlier. This was after he had learned of Montiano's plan to set fire to the Frederica arsenal, blowing up all military stores and ammunition. The blast was to be a signal for the Spanish galleys to come up the river, and in the confusion, land enough men to attack the fort.

The plan was snuffed out. Instead, the Spanish were completely surprised by the vigorous resistance they met from the Frederica cannon. This, added to their land defeat, a serious lack of fresh water, illness from the summer heat, turned the Latins into a complaining, dispirited company. Most alarming to Montiano was the disagreement between his men from St. Augustine and those from Cuba. In bitterness, they had actually moved to separate encampments.

These mounting Spanish misfortunes gave Oglethorpe the advantage he desperately needed. He decided to surround the divided enemy and force surrender. But when he was within two miles of the Spanish encampments, a traitor, who, as a volunteer had worked himself into the General's good graces, betrayed the presence of the British by firing his musket. To make matters worse, he then slipped away to join the enemy. Now Montiano would know Oglethorpe's plans.

Back to Frederica marched the frustrated troops and their leader. How could Oglethorpe make the Spanish distrust the deserter? Why not confuse them with contradictory intelligence? Why not convey that intelligence in a letter supposedly meant for the deserter and send the letter by a Spanish prisoner whom he would release?

Oglethorpe's letter was a masterpiece of subterfuge. It instructed the deserter to convince Montiano of three things: The British forces are disintegrating; this is the time to pilot the Spanish ships up the river toward the fort, bringing them within range of hidden shore batteries; persuade the Spanish to stay for three more days when help will arrive from Carolina—two thousand men by land, seven men-of-war by sea. The letter also suggested that if the deserter succeeded in getting Montiano to believe its contents, there would be a reward "twice what you have already received." Of course, the letter was not signed by Oglethorpe, carefully giving the impression that it was from "a friend."

The released Spanish messenger was seized the moment he returned to his base and taken before General Montiano. When he was searched, the letter was found, and he confessed he had been paid to deliver it to the deserter. Montiano was thoroughly confused. Was the deserter, whom he had paid to spy at Frederica, now spying on him? A double-agent could not be trusted. Were the British weak, or were they stronger than even the fort's guns had hinted? Was he in danger of falling into Oglethorpe's trap?

It was at this time that Governor Bull incidentally sent several ships down the coast to determine whether or not St. Simons harbor was in possession of the Spanish fleet. Of course Montiano did not know they had been ordered to return immediately to Carolina without engaging his navy. He was sure the reinforcements mentioned in the "planted" letter were arriving. The Spaniard dared not gamble his whole army and fleet.

"Embark all troops immediately," he ordered. The ships were loaded in such a hurry that military supplies, cannon, and shot were left on the beach. Those who had died from wounds received in the Battle of Bloody Marsh were forsaken, unburied.

On July 14, the enemy burned the houses they had used on the south end of St. Simons and Jekyll islands. The following day, the ships carrying the Cuban forces put out to sea homeward bound. Montiano, aboard the flagship *Santa Theresa,* led his galleys of Augustines down the inland waterway to land on the northern tip of Cumberland Island. By July 16, Montiano's line of sail appeared off the southern end of Cumberland. There, Ensign Alexander, commander of Fort William, held off the Spanish, repulsing all of their attempts to land troops. With only sixty men Alexander defended the British post. That was when Oglethorpe, in determined pursuit, brought reinforcements to save Fort William. When Montiano saw him coming, he abandoned his final attempt to capture an English garrison. Scout boats ordered by Oglethorpe to track the enemy, returned with the news that they had followed the Spanish all the way to the St. Johns River. By the time armed ships from Carolina finally arrived at Frederica, they were too late—the Spanish were "quite gone."

July 25, 1742, General James Edward Oglethorpe proclaimed a day of thanksgiving, "that the defenders of Frederica might devoutly acknowledge the protecting and favoring providence of God in this wonderful deliverance from a most formidable invading foe."

That the Governor of St. Augustine, with nearly five thousand men under his command, had fled before one hundred Indians and their seven hundred English comrades was an "astonishment."

The colonial governors of Pennsylvania and New York, Maryland and New Jersey, Virginia and North Carolina sent letters to the General "congratulating him upon the important services rendered to the colonies." By saving Georgia he may have saved them all.

One historian claims this victory was as decisive a blow against the Spanish Empire as the battle of Yorktown was to be against the British two decades later.

Chapter 21

IT IS TO Oglethorpe's credit that all of the honor and praise showered upon him did not deflect his caution. His sure instinct told him the Spanish would be back. There was no time to bask in glory or even rest at his Frederica cottage. Once more, he renewed efforts to obtain support from the Crown.

"We have returned thanks to God for our deliverance," he wrote to London. "I have set all hands I possibly could to work upon the fortifications, and am trying to form another battalion. I have retained a gunboat, sent for cannon, shot, provisions, all kinds of stores, since I expect the enemy as soon as they have recovered. They will attack us again with better discipline. I hope that His Royal Majesty will order troops, artillery and other necessities for the defense of this frontier."

The reply? Silence.

By early 1743, intelligence reports proved him right. The Governor-General of Cuba, Guemes y Horcasitas, was recruiting ten thousand men for another attack on Georgia. Surely such a threat would bring assistance from Parliament. Surely now the Carolina Assembly and the Savannah officials would help with defenses. The importance of holding the buffer territory had been proven clearly. Repeatedly, Oglethorpe brought this to the attention of the Duke of Newcastle, who, with his brother, Henry Pelham, had displaced Prime Minister Walpole as leader of the Whigs. "I would not trouble you . . . were it not necessary to prevent future ill consequences by dear bought experiences," Oglethorpe wrote. "Since I am in the midst of the danger here, I can better decide measures for our defense than those at a distance can."

Newcastle, Parliament, even the Georgia Trustees ignored their colonial commander, except to promote him to Brigadier-General.

Whatever could be done to defend Georgia, Oglethorpe knew he must do alone. In March, he decided to go after the Spanish instead of waiting for them to invade St. Simons again. With some four hundred troops, half of them Highlanders and Indians, he sailed with three ships converted into gunboats down the coast to the St. Johns River. There, temporary quarters were set up until the sixty Indians sent ahead brought him information.

Their news was discouraging. St. Augustine was prepared for attack. Help was arriving from Cuba. But Oglethorpe determinedly marched his men thirty-eight miles through swamp, pine forests, and palmetto thickets. Thirst, insects, miasma, heat did not stop them until they were near enough to St. Augustine actually to hear soldiers drilling inside the fort. On the way, forty of the Spanish guards scattered through the woods

116

north of the *castillo* were ambushed and killed by Creek warriors.

"I did all I could to draw the Spanish into action," Oglethorpe wrote on March 21. "I posted grenadiers in ambuscade, advanced myself with a few men in full sight of the town, but they were so meek there was no provoking them." Contemptuous as his words were, he knew the Spaniards did not lack courage. And from their view within the fastness of the Castillo de San Marcos, the General must have cut a ridiculous figure, marching back and forth with his handful of soldiers, challenging his enemies, who were not about to sample such obvious bait. If they ventured out to take the daring General, who knew how many of his troops would rush them? Enough to storm the fort no doubt.

Nothing Oglethorpe did provoked a response from the Spanish. Should he try attacking from the island opposite the *castillo?* That had worked three years ago. First, he sent his rangers and their horses back to St. Johns. Then, taking the rest of the troops with him, he sailed down toward the southern entrance of St. Augustine's harbor, the Matanzas Inlet. But the weather turned against him. The English were unable to go ashore on Anastasia Island. In an open Indian piragua, Oglethorpe reconnoitered the area. Soon he was spotted by three Spanish patrols who shot at him; then a gun in his boat exploded, almost killing him. One report claimed, "Blood gushed from his ears and nose from the shock, but he soon collected himself and cheered up his attendants."

In spite of his awkward luck, Oglethorpe made two important discoveries. A new fort, smaller but patterned after the *castillo,* had been built just inside the mouth of Matanzas Inlet. He was sure it would be

117

manned by expert marksmen. A short distance beyond lay a Spanish man-of-war, its cannon trained on the English ships.

Because of the gales and rough seas, there was no way to maneuver into the harbor even if he dared engage the superior Spanish forces. By March 30, when two more enemy galleys were sighted, Oglethorpe knew his expedition did not have a ghost of a chance. Not only did the Spanish know where he and his men were, there had been ample time for them to send for more help. He had failed again at the scene of his bitterest defeat, St. Augustine.

Reluctantly, he ordered his ships, "Take me back to Frederica." He was tired of trying to defend a colony no one else seemed concerned about. Tired of having risked his life over and over again for a territory that might still be lost. Tired of paying the bills. (He had borne three-quarters of the financial burden of the campaign against the Latins—over 66,000 pounds!)

The month that followed must have been one of soul-searching for Oglethorpe. Since the Battle of Bloody Marsh, he was a military hero, an idol, to many Georgians and Carolinians. To an envious few, he was the object of vilification and loathing. One of his subordinates, whom he had rewarded with promotion, was already in London bringing charges of fraud against him. Lieutenant-Colonel William Cooke was claiming that the General forced his regiment to pay for supplies provided by the Government. The charge was absurd, but reports indicated that the Trustees (who showed such indifference for their general's needs) were listening to Colonel Cooke's complaints. In protest, the Earl of Egmont resigned his powerful office because of "the ill behavior of the Ministry and Parliament with respect to the colony."

The Earl had been Oglethorpe's staunchest friend. Here in America, Bull had once been a friend, too, but now he and Vander Dussen were turning hostile. Added to these woes was the death of Toonahowi, killed in a needless skirmish with the Spanish. By comparison, it seemed almost frivolous that a vagabond Irishman had maliciously blown up the Frederica powder magazine.

It was a despondent General who decided in July to sail for England, leaving behind the colony for which he had sacrificed ten of the best years of his life. He knew he had accomplished the impossible, but what a thankless job.

The only home he had known in America was the one at Frederica under the grove of great live oaks. From its windows, he could see his orchard of ripening oranges, figs, and grapes; the salt marshes ever-changing in the shifting island light. He could see the thriving village of Frederica with a population of nearly one thousand, the fort with its British jack guarding the peaceful river. It was not easy to leave all this. It was not easy to say good-bye to his people here, nor to his comrades in arms—the fierce and tender Highlanders who brought their families from Darien for a last handshake, the Indians who lay gifts of fine hides and handwrought weapons at his feet and silently wept. "We love him," one of the Creek chiefs said. "He does not give us silver, but he has given me the coat off his back, the blanket from under him."

To these, he was still The Great Man, the founder of the English King's last colony in America—the good white Father.

Part Four

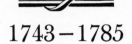

1743–1785

Chapter 22

OGLETHORPE ARRIVED IN London, September 28, 1743, his memory of those Georgia farewells sweet and painful. The Salzburgers, to whom he had given land and freedom of worship, had put him on board the ship *Success* in Charleston. From there, he sailed the Atlantic once more, the Salzburger benediction ever fresh in his thoughts—they had called him "an excellent and blessed instrument of God."

The simplicity of the people he left behind and the spaciousness of their new country made London seem sootier and more strident than he remembered it. The fog and dirt often made it necessary to light candles at ten in the morning. On St. Simons, the autumn winds off the sea were balmy; in London, the shrieking east wind was said to drive some poor souls to suicide. Instead of a mockingbird's glissando at dawn, James was jarred awake by the harsh sounds of wagons and drays on cobblestreets, the yodel of the milk woman who clanked her pails. The din never let up—ships' whistles, bells of the postmen, beggar boys' tambourines and fiddles, sailors and thugs swearing, shouts of "Stop thief!" as pickpockets attacked their victims, the watchman calling out the hour and the state of London's weather. How James hated the thought of approaching winter with its snows wet and deep enough to split trees in two. How he hated the stench of garbage and rotting entrails thrown into the middle of many streets by the butchers.

He must settle his affairs as soon as possible, then go back to Westbrook and Godalming. It would be quiet there.

But it was not until the following year that Oglethorpe was free of two most pressing concerns. It took that long for Parliament to review the accounts of colony expenditures. He had spent 91,705 pounds of his own resources. Until this time, only 25,595 pounds had been repaid. He was relieved to have any part of it restored to his account, even though one member of the House of Commons would not vote without first asking, "What earthly good is this colony of Georgia to us?" The General could not resist reminding his colleagues once more of Georgia's importance to all of the coastal colonies. "The preservation of all of the Crown colonies in America depends on Georgia!"

Was anyone listening? Yes, a few Members of Parliament gave him their attention. He glanced around the chamber at the iron pillars supporting the galleries with their gilded Corinthian capitals (designed by Sir Christopher Wren). They contrasted sharply with the miserable wooden benches upon which some members napped, stretched full-length. Others cracked nuts or sucked oranges, throwing shells and peelings on the floor. Some talked aloud, even violently to young sons they had brought along. The atmosphere scarcely promised Oglethorpe the justice and restitution he sorely needed.

The ordeal of the charges made by Lieutenant-Colonel Cooke must be faced next. The officer's turnabout baffled the General who had gone out of his way to befriend the man, promoting him from Major to Colonel, appointing him chief engineer with extra salary. For thanks, Cooke pleaded illness and left for Charles Town when the Spanish invasion threatened St. Simons. In Carolina, he joined a faction which was trying to discredit Oglethorpe with Parliament. From there, he preceded the General to London where he lodged nineteen charges against his commanding officer. Why?

Oglethorpe asked for a court-martial, but the case was delayed while Cooke pretended he was bringing several witnesses from America. Finally, the Judge Advocate General summoned a Board of General Officers to listen to Cooke's allegations ranging from "unjust impositions" to "an ill state of health" for which he held Oglethorpe responsible.

It was unlikely that an illustrious officer would be found guilty under such circumstances, but the hours of questioning and insults must be endured. For two days, the distinguished board listened to Cooke's charges, then declared them "either frivolous, vexatious or malicious and without foundation."

James Edward Oglethorpe was cleared. Cooke was dismissed from the King's service. At last, the General was free to enjoy the praise of his grateful countrymen. He was the new hero of the Empire. At forty-seven, he had fulfilled brilliantly the roles of parliamentarian, philanthropist, colonial administrator, and military leader. There was little left to challenge his abilities. He could settle down in England to a life befitting his prestige and social rank.

For the first time he realized he needed a wife. The American frontier had demanded too much of him, there had not been time to think of marriage and a family. He remembered with amusement the attention and flirtations of the Carolina ladies, and he enjoyed the pursuit of the single and married women of London. He knew that he was attractive to them all. But it was a little late for courtship and the many risks of love. Besides, Georgia would always be the great romance of his life. All he wanted now was a home and a well-bred wife to preside over it, surrounding him with tranquillity and affectionate companionship.

James must have chosen a bride with the same practical approach with which he had selected the site for Frederica. On September 14, 1744, the office of the Archbishop issued a license to the Honorable James Oglethorpe, Esquire Bachelor, and Elizabeth Wright, Spinster, only daughter of Sir Nathan Wright, Baronet of Cranham, Essex.

The following morning they were married.

Considering Elizabeth Wright's social standing and the groom's fame, it is unlikely that the wedding was a simple affair. When Elizabeth ascended the wide stone steps and passed through the bronze doors into King Henry VIII's glorious chapel at Westminster Abbey, she must have been greeted by the nobility of the Court as well as her groom's associates in the army and Admiralty, government and the arts. A glittering and elite company assembled beneath the ancient, lacy, fan-vaulted roof. Henry VIII's Chapel remains today one of England's most remarkable Gothic treasures, decorated exactly as it was on Oglethorpe's wedding day with the banners, swords, and helmets of the Knights of the Bath—its masonry and richly carved choir stalls unequaled in craftsmanship and elegance.

Since this must have been the wedding of the season,

the magazines and newspapers rhapsodized in prose and poetry, "On the Marriage of General Oglethorpe," and on the honeymoon spent at Westbrook, Surrey. But all of the couple's interests were centered in London, and Lady Oglethorpe's property near Whitehall was an ideal location for their future home.

Chapter 23

BY 1744, THE Jacobite cause stirred scarcely a ripple in the English Parliament. No one there took it seriously any more. In Scotland, it was a different story. The Old Pretender's son, the "Young Chevalier," Charles Edward Stuart, (familiarly known as Bonnie Prince Charlie) was plotting an invasion of Scotland. Once in Scotland, he would rally a following of loyal forces to go on to England where he would claim the throne his exiled father had been denied. On parting from the Old Pretender James, Prince Charlie supposedly said, "I trust, by the aid of God, that I shall soon be able to lay the crowns of Wales and of Scotland and of England at your Majesty's feet."

"Be careful of yourself, my dear boy," the father replied. "I would not lose you for all of the crowns in the world!"

When word reached London that Prince Charlie was in Paris organizing his invasion, the leaders of Parliament were derisive. "He's as near England as he's ever likely to be," they hooted. But by September of 1745, the Jacobites had marched two thousand strong to Edinburgh and had won a battle at Prestonpans. Highlanders flocked to serve the gay and handsome Prince, eager to march across the border into English territory. Five thousand did march as far as Derby, then back again.

The Duke of Cumberland, after whom Oglethorpe named the island off the Georgia coast, was put in command of the English army. The Duke was "a valiant man but inexperienced in war." Despite the Jacobite activities of Oglethorpe's family (his sister, Eleanor de Mézières had continued to support the cause), he was commissioned to raise a regiment which was sent to defend the Yorkshire area where his forefathers had lived. It was there that James converted a number of fox hunters into the Yorkshire Light Horse cavalry "who made more noise than sense."

When intelligence brought word that Bonnie Prince Charlie's invasion of England was set for October 30, Oglethorpe led his troops to Newcastle. There they joined the larger forces of Marshal Wade. A month later, the followers of Prince Charlie were in retreat, and Wade sent Oglethorpe in pursuit with orders to harass the enemy's flank while Wade tried to trap the Prince himself. For four days, Oglethorpe chased the rebels, but at three towns, Preston, Wigan, and Lancaster, he arrived just after they left. Instead of cutting off the retreat of Prince Charlie's rear guard, he let them get away. And in April, when the English finally defeated the Jacobites at Culloden, Scotland, Oglethorpe was not even there. His failure to check the invaders was the only action by his troops that would be remembered. Criticism was severe and widespread. Had Oglethorpe deliberately helped the Jacobite cause? Since fighting side by side with the Scots in Georgia, he had been well known to the Highlanders who organized the rebellion of '45. Was he still loyal to the British Crown, or were his sympathies secretly for the Pretender? Did he help Bonnie Prince Charlie escape to France? Even his friend, the Earl of Egmont, could not be sure.

The Duke of Cumberland had no doubts. He dismissed General Oglethorpe from the commanding staff, and, upon returning to London, instigated a court-martial for the suddenly unpopular veteran. Hour after hour, James Oglethorpe brooded over how swiftly the smiles of fame can become jeers of suspicion and rejection.

From March until September, preparations dragged on for his trial. During this period, Oglethorpe "behaved himself very decently," avoiding public appearances, refusing to discuss the case—certain that his integrity and character would be vindicated.

The warrant read at the opening of the hearings charged him with having "disobeyed or neglected his orders and suffered the rear of the Rebels to escape."

In contrast with the superficial charges of Colonel Cooke, this charge was deadly serious. Oglethorpe was brought into the hearing under arrest, and the most respected generals in the King's service made up the court. After seven days of testimony, he was "most honorably acquitted," in spite of fickle popular support for the Duke of Cumberland. Ironically, Oglethorpe was promoted to full General in time, but he was never again appointed to the top board of officers, which meant he could not serve in any future military activity.

This must have altered his social standing overnight. Instead of being lionized by the blueblood hostesses of London, he and Elizabeth were ignored. The only thing left to him was his office in the House of Commons— he remained the representative from Haslemere. That his post kept him busy, though the assignments were often secondary ones, may have been his salvation, and in time he cultivated additional interests in science and the arts.

In 1749, seven distinguished fellows of the Royal Society sponsored his membership in that august company, describing him as "a gentleman well versed in Natural History, Mathematics and all branches of Polite Literature." While James enjoyed learned conversation with his many friends in the Society, the record shows that he seldom attended meetings and failed to pay his dues.

The President, Sir Hans Sloane, was one of Oglethorpe's closest friends, and when he died, James became an administrator of Sir Hans' vast estate. In this position, he persuaded Parliament to buy Sloane's private collections. The purchase was the beginning of the great British Museum.

Another good friend was Count Zinzendorf. After long talks with Oglethorpe, the Count appealed to Parliament for support of further Moravian immigration to America even though the Moravians were pacifists. It was Oglethorpe who rounded up the votes which passed the Count's philanthropic measure.

While James's interest in Georgia's affairs was as active as ever, he no longer attended meetings of the Trustees. The board had changed not only its membership but its policies. For one thing, they lifted the ban on slavery. James disapproved of the practice more than ever and predicted it would bring only grief to the colony he had founded. On the other hand, he was in favor of the new Georgia representative assembly authorized by the Trustees. Each member of the assembly had been required to plant one hundred mulberry trees on every fifty acres he owned. He was expected to produce fifteen pounds of silk for each fifty acres. At least one female in his family must learn the skill of silk-reeling. At last, the silk industry would be promoted. "It was my idea in the first place," Oglethorpe mused aloud to his wife Elizabeth. "It has taken them all this time to realize how profitable silk can be. But if every member of the Georgia Assembly gets rich from it, what about the other colonists, those who don't own fifty acres? Will they be fairly represented by this new aristocratic class?"

His concern for the poor and for those persecuted because of religious beliefs remained unshaken, and in these more prosperous times—in England and in the self-supporting colony—he reminded his colleagues of the philanthropic origins of Georgia.

Development of the colony was rapid even though many of the idealistic goals of its founder were forgotten. Two thousand people lived in Georgia by 1750, and in 1753 the Trustees asked for a final grant. Through numerous financial crises, they had served honorably, a remarkable feat in an age of corruption. Oglethorpe boasted that the years produced not one charge of fraud or misappropriation of funds. But of Frederica he seldom spoke. Thanks to him, the Spanish were no longer a threat. Frederica had served its strategic purpose and now the settlement there was dwindling. England did not see any point in maintaining the fort, although a small detachment of troops under Captain Raymond Demere remained. Many of the people scattered to the mainland. It was a painful thought for James Edward Oglethorpe. Better that he think of the work at hand.

He plunged into the debates on the Mutiny Bill which

defended the right of noncommissioned soldiers to state complaints and to serve a limited time rather than for life in the King's service. These men, he knew, were always denied unprejudiced investigations. Career general though he was, Oglethorpe lashed out at such injustice. Still quick to stand with the ordinary man when oppressed by the Establishment, he declared, "I shall be jealous of a power, the exercise whereof is trusted to the absolute and arbitrary will of a single man."

But by the time the 1754 elections came around, Oglethorpe's humanity and outstanding accomplishments were scarcely mentioned. Too much the outspoken individualist, he did not fit into the fashionable political mold of bureaucracy. Bureaucracy's servants thought alike, acted alike, and by then its grip on the English Government was firm.

When Parliament was in session, the Oglethorpes lived in London. Otherwise, their time was spent at Mrs. Oglethorpe's country estate in Essex rather than at Westbrook. This also may have influenced the outcome of the Haslemere election that year. The Haslemere representative had performed his duties in the House of Commons, true, but how could he know the concerns of his constituents from such a distance? James must have realized the implications of this failure, because he entered two races—one for the Haslemere seat, the other for Westminster, London. Evidently he believed one or the other community would elect him. Neither did. At first he could not accept the loss and claimed he would contest the results in the Haslemere race, but when he failed to appear at the final hearing, he automatically conceded the election. His long (thirty-two years), productive career in the English Parliament was ended.

That same year, 1754, word got around that the Duke of Cumberland, still the number one military figure, would give the fifty-seven-year-old General an assignment—a new regiment. In that case, Oglethorpe would participate in the Seven Year War which seemed inevitable. But the Duke did not even include Oglethorpe's name on the list of appointments.

Chapter 24

INSTEAD OF MAKING a spectacle of himself over these humiliating dismissals by maneuvering for attention or compelling his associates to tolerate a depressed old has-been, James accepted his fate. He began a leisurely tour of the continent which must have lasted for some time because it was not until 1760 that the still vigorous General and his wife were seen again in London.

In October, George II, while sipping his breakfast chocolate, called to his deaf daughter, Amelia. She could not hear the King, and when she did come to him, he was dead. His grandson became George III.

Oglethorpe, with a sense of foreboding, waited with other Englishmen for the new King's first move. Everyone knew he was a man with definite ideas of his own. Inexperienced and young though he was, he would not be a figurehead. He would rule the Empire. Why, many asked, when he could better leave the job to the capable Secretary of State, William Pitt? Pitt had long given all government orders, had just been credited with winning Canada from the French, shattering France's hopes for an empire in America. Did Pitt's popularity as the "Great Commoner" only increase the determination of George III? Swiftly the King moved personally to dominate the House of Commons. Pitt resigned.

A discarded general knew well how it felt to be a national hero one day, forgotten the next. Oglethorpe wrote to Pitt: "The treatment I met with made me retire from a world that did not want men who preferred the public to their private interest." Oglethorpe, despairing of politics, concluded that individual power was more important these days than the good of the country.

The public heard nothing from him except for occasional letters to editors denouncing practices offensive to his taste or sense of integrity. More and more of his hours were devoted to the people who gave him personal stimulus and pleasure without the stress of competition and intrigue. Men who would become known as the artistic geniuses of that period were far better companions than any politicians: Samuel Johnson and his Boswell, literary celebrities; Dr. Oliver Goldsmith, playwright; David Garrick, stage idol; Edmund Burke, writer, statesman, and critic; Sir Joshua Reynolds, artist (who became the first president of the Royal Academy, and whose portrait, *Samuel Johnson,* is still considered the finest likeness of the famous author).

Oglethorpe in his later years must have been articulate and witty because such men have no time for boredom, and their including him in their select and scholarly circle shows his range of intellectual interests. Gourmands as well as conversationalists of the highest order, these gentlemen were often taken to a chocolate house in their sedan chairs for a noon meeting, followed by a walk in the park, then on to another place for two o'clock dinner, more good talk until six o'clock, tea before the theater, or an evening at the home of a member of the group.

Samuel Johnson undoubtedly dominated these autocrats with his massive physical bulk and raging temperament; he gloried in excess. Though he drank nothing but lemonade during one period, he ate most heartily. If the roast mutton did not come up to Johnson's standards, he would fly into a tirade describing the roast as "bad as bad could be, ill fed, ill killed, ill kept, ill dressed . . ." Immense joints of beef, whole hams, saddles of mutton, fish and meat pies, wild game were served with choice wines and cheeses. The chefs must please the most exotic palates, and Oglethorpe's praise was highly valued. He, the oldest in the circle, was the most temperate, careful of his figure, still slender and as narrow-waisted as a boy.

One day when he was dining at the Smyrna Coffee-House, Boswell whispered to Oglethorpe, "Isn't that your friend, Sir Francis Bernard at the next table?" Boswell knew the very name would incense the old General. "If he is my friend, so is the Devil!" growled Oglethorpe fixing Sir Francis with a hostile stare. "Here I am in the same room with the most despicable colonial governor in British history!"

"Rumor has it, he was recalled from Massachusetts because of his infernal loftiness towards the common citizens, is that so?" Boswell asked slyly.

"They were beneath him if that's what you mean," Oglethorpe snapped. "He has treated the communications of his people with as much indifference as the dust on his boots. Look at that profile, Boswell, a study in arrogance if I ever saw one!"

The next moment, before even Boswell knew what

135

was happening, the General was shaking a bony finger under Sir Francis' nose, shouting, "You're a dirty, factious scoundrel! I smelled your kinship with the hangman when you entered the room, sir. Why, you are not worthy to mix with gentlemen of character, and I am advising you to leave before I show you out!"

Sir Francis' face turned as white as his handsome wig, and with shaking hands, he folded his napkin, stood up uncertainly, and without defending himself by a single word, left the coffee-house. Oglethorpe followed him to the door, then returned to his friends, a look of malicious satisfaction in his gray eyes. "The cur may have the breeding of a racer, but he has the liver of a chicken!"

Already Oglethorpe and Edmund Burke among the select group, were sympathetic to the American colonists in their growing protests against the abuses of the Crown. Neither the King nor Parliament found the grievances of common citizens worth considering. "It is folly and stupidity to fail to listen to them," Oglethorpe warned. "Placing their affairs in the hands of fools like Bernard will lead to rebellion." Oglethorpe knew from firsthand experience that Americans had little time for pomp and ceremony. Their leaders could not stand aloof on grounds of aristocracy or nobility; they must be one of the people, must identify with their hardships and protests. The time would soon pass when a man, simply because he was in the King's favor, could ride to court in a splendid carriage and shut himself away from the people he pretended to serve. "I know the Americans well," the founder of Georgia said. "They will never be subdued by arms; their obedience can be secured only by doing them justice."

Young Boswell, much impressed by the liberal views

136

of his friend, the General, wrote about him in his journals, taking special note of Oglethorpe's kindness to him. Boswell knew it was unusual for a famous man in his sixties to listen so attentively to the theories and complaints of a twenty-year-old. But age was no barrier between them. "I dined at the Oglethorpes' house in Lower Grosvenor Street," the young lawyer wrote. "I felt a completion of happiness—I just sat and hugged myself in my own mind to be in such distinguished company."

The frequent dinner invitations were part of the General's plan to save Boswell from a weakness for drink and pleasure, but Oglethorpe was as concerned with the youth's career as with his character. When Boswell was called to court one morning at the unearthly hour of eight o'clock on his first important case, the General "with the activity of a young soldier and the zeal of a warm friend" attended him. Whether as barrister or author, Boswell received such encouragement from their first meeting.

"I cannot imagine why some people call the General a relic of a more chivalrous century . . . an antique," Boswell said. "His curiosity and spirit are as fresh as my own."

Oglethorpe's gaunt, skeletonlike figure caused speculation about his age, but his mind was vigorous, flexible, his recall of youthful military exploits accurate in surprising detail. "Tell us about Prince Eugene and the siege of Belgrade," begged the admiring Boswell. Then the General would sketch the lines of battle on the tablecloth and describe the action, but the sketch was not as vivid as his words. To Boswell, the old man was a great storyteller, his sense of drama and suspense superb.

"Why not let me preserve these anecdotes for posterity?" Samuel Johnson asked the General one day. "Your biography would be a gift to the world."

"The life of a private man is not worth publication," Oglethorpe replied, dismissing the suggestion, but a little later he said to Boswell, "Perhaps you could bring me a good almanac which would help me recollect dates." Whether or not he recorded his memoirs, nothing ever came of the biography although Johnson made notes from time to time.

This explains why there is no record of conversations with the Wesleys when they renewed their friendship with the General. He saw them at concerts and meetings and took a keen interest in Charles Wesley's sons who were talented musically. He also went to Charles's home on Sunday afternoons when the illustrious John sometimes spoke on a biblical text and led his audience in the simple hymns based on his brother's poems.

John and Charles Wesley could no longer be criticized as in the early days of the Georgia colony for their cold and spiritless religious form. Oglethorpe was glad to discover how warm they now were, and that they included people of all classes in their gatherings. Both talked of their conversion from sterile theology to heart-changing truth, and the change must have been most evident to Oglethorpe who had known them all of their lives.

The General's own faith was as simple as a child's, more evident in attitudes than in words. His habit of reading from the Bible was known to all of his intimate friends, and he delighted in writing out prayers of majestic praise and gratitude. (The more formal ones amounted to lengthy documents.)

Along with Wesley hymns, Oglethorpe learned Oliver Goldsmith's ballads from plays such as *She Stoops to Conquer.* He also shared Dr. Goldsmith's interest in medicine and was a charter contributor to the Children's Hospital.

During summer visits to Mrs. Oglethorpe's estate in Cranham, Essex, and on overseeing trips to Westbrook, Oglethorpe, the landowner, offered loans to those tenants unable to pay their rent. When their crops were harvested, they could repay him, he said. That touch with the ordinary workman for which he was beloved in Georgia had not changed.

Chapter 25

IN THE SPRING of 1775, James returned to London in time to give a dinner, an annual tradition, for his circle of friends. It was their first meeting since the recent death of Goldsmith and they all missed the doctor. As usual, the conversation was monopolized by Samuel Johnson who, with Boswell, had journeyed to the Hebrides. With gusto, Johnson told of his travels, ridiculed his own attempts at dancing, discoursed on Abyssinians, and revealed that some of his writing had been sent to America for the first time. "An Englishman cannot expect a cordial reception there," he said, shifting his great bulk away from the banquet table. "They will in all probability hang me in effigy as they have the Crown's representative from Boston's Liberty Tree!"

This was only nine days before the fighting at Lexington and Concord. "The American colonists are infected with a fever of rebellion," Johnson continued.

"They are not a nation—they owe allegiance to the Crown, and that includes paying taxes as does the rest of the Empire."

"Is taxation the issue?" Oglethorpe asked, a twinkle in his eye. "I heard it was taxation without representation. The King cannot expect to go on robbing the colonists of that basic right as he did in the case of the infamous Stamp Act. They are going to defend their civil liberties with force if necessary."

"The King is stupid," Boswell said in disgust.

"I gather you gentlemen will not approve the paper I am working on, *Taxation no Tyranny*," Samuel Johnson said, his face florid with anger. "The authority of the Crown cannot be subject to mob approval I say!"

"I say the King is foolish to ignore the colonists' Declaration of Rights," Oglethorpe responded. "Anyone who knows what settling a frontier is all about must agree that the Americans are entitled to life, liberty and property, and they are not going to give to any sovereign power the right to dispose of those most precious possessions without their consent!"

It was just as well that Johnson and Boswell were too busy in the months that followed for more discussions with Oglethorpe. His sympathy for the American colonies, particularly his favorites, Carolina and Georgia, marked him "for the cause," and he found it easier to talk with Edmund Burke who agreed with him, and with Granville Sharp, the scholar-abolitionist, who shared his hatred of slavery.

The General was seventy-eight when the American Revolution began. He knew every battle by 1778 as though he had plotted it. He studied every resolution,

140

every declaration that came out of the Continental Congress as though they were products of his own mind.

With Granville Sharp, he made one last attempt at influencing their friends in government towards conciliation with the Americans instead of final alienation. It was too late.

The next year, David Garrick died. The makeup of the intellectual circle was changing but not Oglethorpe's enthusiasm for the War of American Independence. At Garrick's funeral, the circle of friends was called the Literary Club, and became organized under that name. Could the aging General's delight in the Americans' final victory over the British have been the reason he was not listed as a charter member in the new club?

Boswell spent much of his time in Edinburgh; Johnson was buried in an ambitious writing project. They now seldom saw Oglethorpe, but on one visit to London, Boswell observed, "The General seems much older and visibly failing." Looks were deceiving. Boswell could not keep up with Oglethorpe who took him on a round of parties and sessions of Parliament.

He could outwalk anyone fifty years his junior, and, at two o'clock in the morning was still talking brilliantly while Boswell nodded. At eighty-seven, he was described as "alert, upright, has his eyes, ears and memory fresh." London's society hostesses competed for his company. The poetess Hannah More, still in her thirties, called him her "new admirer" and flirted with him publicly. "He is the finest figure you ever saw," Hannah wrote her sister. "He is quite a *preux chevalier*, heroic, romantic, and full of the old gallantry."

Hannah was not the only young woman charmed by

James Edward Oglethorpe in his great age. Others discussed his remarkable daily exercise, impressed apparently by the fact that he walked and shot with the Finsbury Archers "with his waistcoat almost entirely unbuttoned in the middle of winter."

No one was surprised that he survived the corpulent Samuel Johnson who died on December 13, 1784. Nor were they surprised when the General turned up in Christie's galleries two months later for the auctioning of Johnson's library. Already Christie's was attracting leading book and art dealers from all over the world, and it was a meeting place for intelligentsia.

Moving among them with ease, the legendary, imposing General studied his catalog and estimated that the Johnson sale would last four days. During that time, an artist did a pen-and-ink sketch of James in his beribboned tricorn and stylish skirted coat. The huge cuffs turned back from white linen ruffles fall over his gnarled hands. His legs are lean and youthful in tight-fitting breeches and stockings. At his side is the sword his father gave him.

In June of 1785, the newspapers screamed disapproval of King George III for receiving at the Court of Saint James the first high ranking official representative from the United States of America. The ambassador was John Adams. The meeting between the two bold and stubborn men made headlines and stirred English resentment. Especially did the public deplore the King's warm response to Adams when he said, "I must say that I not only receive with pleasure the assurance of the friendly dispositions of the United States, but that I am glad the choice has fallen upon you to be their

142

minister . . ." Wasn't it bad enough for His Royal Majesty to speak those words "United States" without expressing goodwill toward the very rebel who helped the American colonies win independence from the most powerful empire in the world?

Three days after John Adams' audience with King George, while editors still raged and the public sputtered, Oglethorpe walked over to the new legation on Grosvenor Square and presented his card to the American ambassador, who must have been delighted by then to see a friendly British face.

"I have come to pay my respects to the first American Ambassador and his family." The old General spoke, simply.

John Adams gestured toward a chair, but Oglethorpe said, "Let me finish first, sir. What I have to say is very important to me. I am glad to see you in England, and to learn that in one cordial meeting you have already dispelled our monarch's long-standing hostility." The old man smiled. "I suppose I need not try to express to you my great esteem and affection for America, Mister Adams."

"No, General Oglethorpe, you are remembered by all our states as are your exploits in founding the great colony of Georgia." John Adams looked into Oglethorpe's faded gray eyes. "Americans will forever consider you one of us in the defense of freedom and opportunity for all mankind."

The General sank into the chair the American ambassador offered and leaned his head against the high back.

"I have regretted the misunderstanding between our countries, as you know, Adams."

143

"Yes, sir, I know."

"And I am very happy," Oglethorpe said, "to have lived to see the end of it."

As though there was no further happiness he could ever desire, James Edward Oglethorpe died within the month, June 30, 1785.

R0127666217 sscca S B
035B

Blackburn, Joyce
James Edward Oglethorpe

R0127666217 sscca S B
035B

Houston Public Library
Social Sci